The Roman Remains

John Izard Middleton,
Interior of the Coliseum by night (Plate #17)

The Roman Remains

John Izard Middleton's Visual Souvenirs
of 1820–1823

with Additional Views in Italy,
France, and Switzerland

Edited with Essays and Catalogue Commentary by Charles R. Mack
and Lynn Robertson, including an Appreciation of the Artist first
published in 1885 by Charles Eliot Norton

Complementary photography by Charles R. Mack

PUBLISHED BY THE UNIVERSITY OF SOUTH CAROLINA PRESS FOR THE SOUTH
CAROLINIANA LIBRARY WITH THE ASSISTANCE OF THE CAROLINE MCKISSICK DIAL
PUBLICATION FUND AND THE UNIVERSITY CAROLINIANA SOCIETY

Copyright © 1997 University of South Carolina

Published in Columbia, South Carolina, by the
University of South Carolina Press

Manufactured in the United States of America

01 00 99 98 97   5 4 3 2 1

Library of Congress Cataloging-in-Publication Data

Middleton, John Izard, 1785–1849.
   The Roman remains : John Izard Middleton's visual souvenirs of
1820–1823, with additional views in Italy, France, and Switzerland /
edited with essays and catalogue commentary by Charles R. Mack and
Lynn Robertson, including an appreciation of the artist first
published in 1885 by Charles Eliot Norton; complementary
photography by Charles R. Mack.
      p.   cm.
   Includes bibliographical references and index.
   Norton's appreciation of Middleton, "The first American classical
archaeologist," originally appeared in v. 1, no. 1, of the American
Journal of Archaeology in 1885.
   ISBN 1–57003–169–X (cloth)
   1. Rome Region (Italy)—Antiquities. 2. Rome Region (Italy)—
Antiquities—Pictorial works. 3. Middleton, John Izard, 1785–1849—
Contributions in archaeology. 4. Archaeologists—United States—
Biography. 5. Artists—United States—Biography. 6. Rome (Italy)—
Intellectual life—19th century. I. Mack, Charles R., 1940– .
II. Robertson, Lynn, 1947– . III. Norton, Charles Eliot,
1827–1908. First American classical archaeologist. IV. Title.
DG63.M63 1997
937—dc21   97–4726

In memory of my grandmother, Anna Finck Dirnberger, who first came to Rome in 1957 at the age of seventy-nine and who, as "Mrs. D.," was an active part of its scene for five happy years.

Charles R. Mack

In memory of my mother, Patricia Martin Robertson, who, as an artist, taught me to appreciate the unique beauty in drawings.

Lynn Robertson

CANTO IV, lxxviii

Oh Rome! my country! city of the soul!
The orphans of the heart must turn to thee,
Lone mother of dead empires! and control
In their shut breasts their petty misery.
What are our woes and sufferance? Come and see
The cypress, hear the owl, and plod your way
O'er steps of broken thrones and temples, Ye!
Whose agonies are evils of a day—
A world is at our feet as fragile as our clay.

Lord Byron,
Childe Harold's Pilgrimage, 1817

Contents

Foreword

The publication of John Izard Middleton's *The Roman Remains* is the third in a series of books highlighting some of the vast manuscript collections held by the South Caroliniana Library at the University of South Carolina. The Library is proud to maintain one of the finest research collections on the American South, especially materials related to South Carolina. The publication of these volumes by the University of South Carolina Press is made possible by the Caroline McKissick Dial endowment. This fund was established to honor one of the University's most memorable first ladies, who also was the last surviving founder of the South Caroliniana Society. The intent of the endowment is to make items in the South Caroliniana Library's collections, such as *The Roman Remains*, more accessible not only to scholars but to a wider community as well.

The University of South Carolina was established in 1801 to unify the state's lowcountry and upcountry societies. Although it was established in the center of the state, the University has always maintained close ties to the lowcountry and, in fact, John Drayton of Charleston, as governor, was instrumental in the founding of the University. Several lowcountry figures made significant contributions to our Library's early collection. John Izard Middleton, who produced this manuscript in the 1820s, also had strong ties to the South Carolina lowcountry. He was a member of the powerful Middleton family and son of Arthur Middleton, a delegate to the Continental Congress and a signer of the Declaration of Independence. This volume is just another fine example of the significant research materials housed in the South Caroliniana Library. The Library also has the distinction of being the oldest free-standing library in the United States.

George D. Terry
Vice Provost and Dean of Libraries and Information Systems
University of South Carolina

Acknowledgments

I am grateful to both George D. Terry, Vice Provost and Dean of Libraries and Information Systems, and Allen Stokes, Director of the South Caroliniana Library, for offering me the opportunity of becoming involved with this literary and artistic adventure. Catherine Fry, Director of the University of South Carolina Press, greeted this project with enthusiasm and was most supportive during its evolution. I am indebted to Barbara Doyle of the Middleton Place Foundation for sharing her knowledge of John Izard Middleton's life and for her kindness in reviewing portions of this manuscript. In Rome I enjoyed the cooperation of Fr. Anthony J. Grimshaw, Director, The Venerable English College Palazzola, and of the librarians of the Bibliotheca Hertziana, and the advice of Professor Philipp Fehl and his wife, Raina.

The assistance of John O'Neil, the former chair of my department, in the form of an Assigned Time for Research Grant in the summer of 1995 that enabled me to complete most of the writing of my portion of the essays and entries is gratefully acknowledged. A travel grant from the Samuel H. Kress Foundation made possible a trip to Rome in March 1996 to complete necessary research and to execute the photographs that complement many of the Middleton drawings. Gordon Brown of the McKissick Museum greatly enhanced my feeble photographic skills through his skillful developing and printing. These photographs both prove the accuracy of John Izard Middleton's eye and illustrate the effects of 175 years of a changing environment. The assistance of Peggy Nunn in preparing this manuscript was invaluable. And thanks are due also to Phil H. Sawyer, Jr., of the University of South Carolina Instructional Support Department, for copy photography of Middleton's drawings.

I am pleased to credit the resources of the Thomas Cooper Library of the University of South Carolina. In Middleton's day, my university, then called South Carolina College, was one of America's premier institutions of higher learning, and the collection of nineteenth-century guidebooks and related materials it acquired made my selection of quotations for this volume a far easier task than it might have been and kept interlibrary loans to a minimum.

Throughout the project I have enjoyed the enthusiastic cooperation of my co-editor, Lynn Robertson. She is responsible for the bulk of the archival research that has helped to illuminate the life of Mr. Middleton. A special note of appreciation must go to my wife, Ilona, for her many comments and suggestions along the way and for her great patience and calming presence when, late one Tuesday night, my computer crashed along with half of what was an all but completed text for much of this book aboard—a total wipeout, inadequately compensated by a much out-of-date back-up disk. It was one of the worst experiences of my academic life. I have learned a great deal in the preparation of this publication (much done twice over). I have learned about nineteenth-century art and literature, the archaeological appreciation of ancient Rome, the interaction of America with its European heritage, and, above all, to make daily back-up copies of whatever I have entered into the computer.

A final debt of gratitude goes to my colleague Professor David Rembert and his wife, Margaret, who with F. Dean Rainey brought John Izard Middleton's remarkable volume of drawings into the care of the South Caroliniana Library. Their gift has rescued from oblivion not only forty-nine splendid views of early-nineteenth-century Italy and Savoy but also has given new recognition to a significant American artist and scholar. The publication of Middleton's *Roman Remains* will most certainly prove of lasting value to all who enjoy the Italian scene and honor those who have helped create our memory of it. I am hopeful that it eventually will provoke a monographic treatment of the artist whose fascinating life we can but barely survey in the following essays.

Charles R. Mack

I wish to add my acknowledgment of appreciation to Allen Stokes, Director of the South Caroliniana Library and University Librarian for Special Collections, for providing Dr. Mack and me with such a wonderful set of drawings with which to work. He and George D. Terry, Vice Provost and Dean of Libraries and Information Systems, have guided this project with enthusiasm and institutional support from its inception.

As Charles R. Mack points out, we owe an immense amount of gratitude to Margaret Rembert and F. Dean Rainey, who saw to it that this remarkable book of drawings found its way into such a distinguished and public library.

I want to thank Barbara Doyle of the Middleton Place Foundation for her hours of patience in guiding me through the complex but fascinating Middleton family genealogy. She also graciously read parts of the manuscript to assure us that we had all of our cousins, nieces, brothers, and uncles correctly identified and in the right place at the right time. She and the other staff members of Middleton Place have been very helpful in fulfilling our desire to see what few other John Izard Middleton works exist. Alex Moore, Director of the South Carolina Historical Society, also provided much assistance with those Middleton papers housed at that institution. Henry Fulmer, Manuscript Librarian at the South Caroliniana Library, guided me through other Middleton holdings.

This manuscript would not have been produced without the help of Peggy Nunn, who assembled the many parts and versions of our text as well as expertly proofread each of the revisions. Gordon Brown photographed the drawings and worked long hours to capture Middleton's delicate pencil and pen strokes.

Finally, thank you to Charles Randall Mack, who made my foray into the world of nineteenth-century travel and learning both exciting and rewarding at each step of the project. His deep enthusiasm for the history of art is always a source of inspiration for me.

Lynn Robertson

The Roman Remains

Introduction

Charles R. Mack

"Now, at last, I have arrived in the First City of the world." These words were penned by Johann Wolfgang von Goethe when he arrived in Rome from Germany in 1786. Goethe's emotion was what I, too, felt when I first came to Rome as an American teenager in 1957. Rome was to be my on-and-off home for the next five years. Little more than a decade after World War II, Rome was experiencing tremendous change. The cardboard communities of refugee *contadini* still lined the ancient Aurelian walls near the Porta Maggiore, but vast expanses of sterile, high-rise apartment blocks were being readied on the outskirts, the dehumanizing character of the structures later depicted with stark beauty in Federico Fellini's *La Dolce Vita*. And Rome's decade-long romance with the "Sweet Life" had commenced along the short stretch of the café-lined Via Veneto between the American Embassy and the Pincian Gate leading out of the old city. Here thronged the moviemakers and the "want-to-be's," the diplomats, the writers, the designers, and the onlookers; here strutted the peacocks and the paparazzi. Rome was certainly a city of great contrast: ancient grandeur and modern fashion, communist demonstrators and film stars, flashy cars and grinding poverty, deep cynicism and much idealism—an inflammatory mix that eventually would explode into the Red Brigade violence of the 1970s. It was an exciting time to be living in Rome.

On her visit to Italy in 1804–5, Madame de Staël wrote of "the barren countryside surrounding Rome, which is not arid but which seems to mourn its former owners." The romance of the Roman Campagna depicted in many a Dutch Romanist's painted baroque *veduta* (view) and, later, in John Izard Middleton's spare lines was still to be seen in the mid twentieth century, but suburban sprawl was already beginning a relentless encroachment. In many ways, and with little exaggeration, there is more resemblance between the Roman region that I first encountered and Middleton's views drawn almost a century and a half earlier than there is with what one finds today. Much of the magic of Rome and its Campagna has vanished in the last three decades. Even as early as the late 1950s people were starting to complain about the traffic and the pollution, but these were nothing compared to what they had become when I next lived in Rome only ten years later, and today, well—it is better left unsaid and, often, untried.

In the late 1950s, once one drove past the new residential quarter of Vigna Clara along the Via Cassia, the old road, aside from its blacktop paving and annoying Vespa motor scooters, must have been much as the nineteenth-century traveler had known it. Middleton and his contemporaries would have recognized the little communities along its course—Tomba di Nerone, la Storta, Isola Farnese. The pasturelands and plowed fields covering the ancient site of Etruscan Veii in 1957 would have been familiar to the first great generation of Etruscologists, including William Gell, Antonio Nibby, and George Dennis. Not so today. The apartment houses of suburban Rome look to besiege the city's old rival. One is reminded of Suetonius's ancient jest about the emperor Nero's celebrated Golden House: "All Rome is transformed into a Villa! Romans, flee to Veii, if only the villa does not also spread itself to Veii!" Centuries later the Neronian nightmare seems to be coming true. The same, to one degree or another, goes for the sites Middleton drew for his projected second volume of views published here as *The Roman Remains*: Albano, Castel Gandolfo, Ariccia, Ardea. Much of the mystery and celebrity of the ruins he depicted also have been lost. Who really visits the so-called Tomb of the Horatii and Curiatii? Who, today, knows enough Livy to honor the tomb's memory? Does the Tomb of the Scipios today conjure up the visions of republican patriotism that it did for Lord Byron and, obviously, for our English-schooled and cosmopolitan artist from South Carolina?

John *Izard* Middleton

His Life and Art

Charles R. Mack and Lynn Robertson

"The first American classical archaeologist" was the term used to describe John Izard Middleton in 1885 by Charles Eliot Norton, at the time one of the foremost cultural historians in the United States and Harvard University's first professor of fine arts. Middleton had earned Norton's accolade for his *Grecian Remains in Italy: A Description of Cyclopian Walls and of Roman Antiquities, with Topographical and Picturesque Views of Ancient Latium*, published in London beginning in 1812. The volume was an extraordinary, folio edition of twenty-two colored aquatints and two plates of line engravings based upon the young artist's on-site drawings of antiquities in central Italy executed in 1808 and 1809. It is Middleton's probable intended sequel to that endeavor, produced a decade and a half later, that now receives its initial publication as *The Roman Remains*.

John Izard Middleton was born at Middleton Place on the Ashley River near Charleston, South Carolina, on 13 August 1785. Known always as Izard (although he signed himself J. I. Middleton), he was the second son and youngest child of Arthur Middleton and Mary Izard. His was a wealthy family firmly established among the political and social leaders of the new nation. Arthur Middleton had himself been born at Middleton Place in 1742 while his father (Henry Middleton) was establishing the plantation's famous gardens. He was forty-three at the time of John Izard's birth and recognized as a patriot. Like most wealthy young men in the South Carolina colony, Arthur Middleton was educated in England. He returned to South Carolina on Christmas Eve, 1763, and the following summer married Mary Izard, the daughter of the prosperous merchant, planter, and family friend Walter Izard. In 1768 the couple traveled to England and the Continent for a grand tour, during which their first child, Henry, was born. In 1771 they had their portrait painted in London by Benjamin West before sailing back to Charleston, never to return to England. Arthur Middleton became immersed in the politics of revolution, and his dedication to American independence earned him the epithet of "radical" from his fellow planters. He was elected to the Second Continental Congress and signed the Declaration of Independence. During the Revolution he continued in Congress and served in the defense of Charleston. After the fall of the city in 1780 he was arrested by the British and imprisoned at Saint Augustine until the end of the war. He returned to Middleton Place, where he remained as a gentleman farmer until his death in 1787 at the age of forty-five from an unspecified fever, probably malaria. Arthur Middleton's vast fortunes, including Middleton Place and the Newport estates, were passed on to his eldest son, Henry, who was only seventeen at the time of his father's death. Although Henry divided his time between Rhode Island and South Carolina, his mother remained at her Charleston home.

At Middleton Place, Izard grew up in cultured surroundings. The gardens were enlarged, and André Michaux, the French botanist, introduced a number of new and rare plants on his visit to the plantation. The house, according to a *Charleston Courier* description of 1840, was "decorated with numerous paintings, portraits, and historical and fancy pieces." Some of these items, no doubt, had been added by Henry Middleton, who, after serving as legislator, governor, and congressman, traveled in Europe from 1820 to 1830 while he served as the American minister to Russia. However, much of the original art collection, furnishings, and library, we might suppose, were acquired by Arthur Middleton and his young wife on their extensive pre-Revolutionary travels in England and Italy. According to the later recollections of a distant cousin, Alicia Hopton Middleton, in her *Life in Carolina*: "The walls of the library [of Middleton Place] above the wainscot were lined with well-filled book shelves; below were closets and drawers full of rare works of art, watercolors of unusual size, priceless engravings, exquisite miniatures and other treasures, ten thousand in all, it was said, the collection of many generations of travel in Europe and distant lands" (p. 65). Whatever the contents of Middleton Place during Izard's childhood, this noble collection, proof of the taste, wealth, and cosmopolitan character of this family of South Carolina aristocrats, largely disappeared when Union troops sacked and burned the residence in 1865. The central portion of the house and its library wing were consumed and most of the contents destroyed or dispersed. Even without the tangible evidence, however, it is clear that the young John Izard Middleton was immersed in a world that valued learning and good taste. He had at his disposal the resources through which he could prepare himself for his later scholarly and social pursuits.

Like Arthur Middleton, who attended Cambridge University, young Izard was sent to England for his education and attended Trinity College at Cambridge from 1801 to 1803. The citation in John Archibald Venn's *Alumni Cantabrigienses* (p. 181) indicates that Izard Middleton was graduated at age nineteen and probably did not reside at the college during his studies. A purported silhouette portrait of the young Middleton, now in the collection at Middleton Place, shows him in his academic gown as a fellow commoner. Once abroad, his father had studied the classics and art, and so, apparently, did Izard. The Middleton fortune and the considerable Izard family resources from his mother allowed him to travel and pursue the life of leisure and learning among the upper echelon of the European intelligentsia. The extensive connections within the Middleton family to England and the Continent placed him within familiar circles, and he no doubt frequently saw friends and relatives visiting from the United States. In 1794 his brother, Henry, had married Mary Hering of Bath, England. Her mother's correspondence of 1801 records one of the earliest impressions of Izard as a popular and lively guest among the Hering family and friends. He seems to have been at home in England, France, and Italy, moving with apparent ease through languages and cultures. Norton's centenary article in the *American Journal of Archaeology* noted that Middleton "was received . . . in circles into which foreigners seldom gained entrance."

Silhouette of John Izard Middleton in academic dress, ca. 1803. From the permanent collection of the Middleton Place Foundation, Charleston, South Carolina.

To date, John Izard Middleton has never been the subject of a biographical monograph, and, strangely, no personal journals or diaries and little correspondence have been found. The present sketch of his life is intended only as an attempt to provide a personal context in which the viewer might better regard this recently discovered album of drawings; his life is certainly deserving of more intense study. That effort is currently under way and will, it is hoped, lead to the publication of a monograph devoted to Middleton's life and artistic career. His character and the events of his life must be reconstructed through passing references in the writings of his contemporaries and in the letters of family members who visited him in Europe or who exchanged information about him. A clear chronology of the events of Izard's life is hampered by the fact that his brother, Henry, named his fourth son (born in 1800) after him, and it is sometimes difficult to distinguish which John Izard is meant in public accounts. Generally, it would seem, Henry's son was referred to as John.

Alicia Hopton Middleton, writing her reminiscences, described John Izard Middleton as "the intimate friend" of both Anne-Louise Germaine Necker, baronne de Staël-Holstein, the celebrated writer and arbiter of intellectual taste better known as Madame de Staël, and Madame Juliette Récamier, whose legendary beauty can be appreciated in the two famous portraits of her in Paris, one by Jacques-Louis David (1800) in the Louvre and the other by François Gérard (1802).

The known association between Middleton and Madame de Staël's circle has been used as the basis for reconstructing something of Middleton's character and his artistic initiation. According to this theory, Middleton either traveled with Staël to Italy or fell into her company in Rome. Germaine de Staël's Italian journey produced, of course, her celebrated romance, *Corinne, or Italy* (published in Paris in 1807), described by one of her biographers, Christopher Herold, as "the worst great novel ever written"; critics have suggested that Middleton's presence can be detected lurking within the personality of the book's male protagonist, the equivocating Oswald Lord Nelvil. The assumption upon which these attractive suggestions have been predicated is that Middleton was among Staël's attendants on her trip to Italy, remaining there to execute the drawings for his *Grecian Remains*.

Despite this romantic hypothesis, what is documented indicates otherwise. Madame de Staël made her tour in the period from December 1804 to June 1805, and there is no evidence to indicate that Middleton either accompanied her on this trip or was in Rome at the time (he would have been but nineteen) or that he had even, as yet, encountered Staël. Her companions on this trip were August Wilhelm von Schlegel (the translator of Shakespeare into German) and the Swiss historian Jean Charles Sismondi. Far from including Middleton's personality in his character, Staël's Oswald Nelvil is actually based upon a composite of two of her lovers, Dom Pedro de Souza of Portugal and Prosper de Barante.

In actuality, Middleton was not introduced into Staël's presence until the summer of 1807, when he was among an illustrious company of guests brought together at her Château de Necker outside the village of Coppet, situated on the northwestern shore of Lake Leman in Switzerland. Among the group assembled by Madame de Staël were many of her friends, former lovers, and admirers, including Benjamin Constant, Schlegel, Sismondi, Karl Victor von Bonstettin, Barante, Mathieu de Montmorency, and Prince Augustus of Prussia. The French portraitist Elisabeth Vigée-Lebrun was also among the guests. Staël served as the intellectual stimulus of this Swiss summer, but its amorous catalyst was Madame Juliette Récamier. At thirty, Madame Récamier was still regarded as the most seductive temptress on the Continent.

The young Middleton may have been fascinated by Staël's conversation, but he apparently was enamored by Récamier's flirtatious beauty. Unfortunately, it was the Prussian Prince Augustus who captured Récamier's eye. Récamier must have fueled Middleton's infatuation, however, for after she had left Coppet in October, Staël wrote to her on 2 December that Middleton had "sobbed with grief" at her departure. In a letter of 25 June 1808 quoted in Edouard Herriot's *Madame Récamier*, Staël posed a question to Récamier involving Middleton: "What are you going to do with Prince Augustus and with Middleton?" and then encouraged the beauty to "give me your orders, dear sovereign, as regards this" and noted that she suspected "that there is someone you like very much. Tell me whether I am mistaken. I am quite ready to receive him [at Coppet] and to console the dead and wounded" (vol. I, p. 184).

Middleton, in fact, had left Coppet shortly after Récamier's departure, heading south over the Alps, to make the same voyage of Italian discovery that Staël had made three years earlier. His travels were, perhaps, motivated by his hostess's *Corinne,* which had just been published and which, it is known, had stimulated much of the conversation that summer. Writing to Récamier from Vienna early in 1808, Staël noted that she had received letters from Middleton from Italy, and in July, Staël, writing from Coppet, informed Récamier that she had heard that Middleton was in Rome, where he was "in love with an American woman who was not very worthy of him" (Herriot, pp. 185–86). Other letters from Staël note Middleton's additional involvement with Ida Brun (later the countess de Bombelles), the daughter of Madame de Staël's friend the Danish poetess Frederika Brun. Madame de Staël was not the only person to correspond with Récamier. Though they are now lost, pieces of Middleton family correspondence sometimes mention "Récamier letters." The last reference to those letters is in correspondence from Williams Middleton, who witnessed the Civil War destruction of his Middleton Place, to Henry Middleton in 1870.

Portrait of Juliette Récamier, 1808, copied by Pierre-Narcisse Guérin from the original by François Gérard. From the permanent collection of the Middleton Place Foundation, Charleston, South Carolina.

Dalliance with American and Danish women and what we might suspect was a taste for *la dolce vita* were not Middleton's only pursuits on his visit to Italy in 1807–9. During his initial Italian travels, Middleton most likely would also have encountered fellow South Carolinian Washington Allston, five years his senior, who in 1808 was completing a four-year artist's residency in Rome. Allston had studied painting in London between 1801 and 1803, and it is at least conceivable that the two had met there. Middleton would, unfortunately, have missed meeting Allston's colleague, the French-trained American painter John Vanderlyn, who had left Rome just before his arrival. Like Madame de Staël's fictional Oswald Nelvil, Middleton "awoke in Rome . . . [and] opened his eyes to a dazzling sun, an Italian sun, and his soul was filled with loving gratitude to a heaven that seemed revealed in its radiant beams" (*Corrine,* p. 9). The academic as well as the artistic certainly ran strong in the young Middleton, and he apparently kept up with the latest in classical scholarship. The conflict between England and France clearly did not keep him from perusing the scholarly writings of the French architect Louis-François Petit-Radel (1740–1818), whose interpretations of antiquity were to influence his own course of investigation. His antiquarian forays into the hill country south of Rome also may have been inspired by the book on Latium published in 1805 by Bonstettin, the Swiss writer and philosopher and one of his fellow houseguests at Coppet in 1807.

During this visit to Rome, Middleton evidently made the acquaintance of Edward Dodwell (1767–1832), newly arrived from an excursion to Greece, and it was in his company that the young South Carolinian set out to wander the Alban hills and the countryside south of Rome searching for what was then thought to be the tangible remains of a mysterious pre-Roman civilization called the Pelasgian, about whose existence Petit-Radel had theorized. Dodwell, whose book *Classical and Topographical Tour through Greece* was to be published in London in 1819, may have encouraged the young American along the way to use his artistic talents for drawing. In any case Middleton would have found truth in the words of a later traveler to the region, the Reverend John A. Clark, who discovered that "It is impossible to live in Italy long without becoming at least a profound amateur in the fine arts" (*Glimpses of the Old World*, vol. I, p. 302).

The visual record of Middleton's first encounter with the wonders of ancient Italy was published in London as the *Grecian Remains*. Although Middleton composed a descriptive text for his volume, he made it quite clear that it was the archaeological accuracy of his visual renditions that gave the book its distinction. He noted the futility of verbal descriptions of monuments for which there was no ancient literary guide, for "the local evidence is [often] in contradiction with the testimony of the [modern] historian," a situation that forced him to conclude that "in a tour of this kind, the artist is perhaps of more real use than the scholar; and after toiling through the obscure pages of an historian, I found that my sketch told me more than my notes. I for this reason adopted the plan of making a collection of very accurate drawings."

Middleton stated that his on-site renditions were executed in the company of two Englishmen and that the *Grecian Remains* actually incorporated a few of the drawings of one of these companions. He acknowledged as his, "the original outlines of the eighteenth, nineteenth, twentieth, twenty-eighth, and thirty-fifth plates." As the published volume presented only twenty-two views, Middleton must initially have intended a more expansive publication, an intent preserved in the words of his text.

The several drawings borrowed by Middleton for his volume most likely came from the hand of Edward Dodwell. Dodwell's later archaeological distinction was based not only upon his 1818 guide to Greece but also upon his own *Views and Descriptions of Cyclopian, or, Pelasgic Remains in Greece and Italy; with Constructions of a Later Period* (published posthumously in 1834 in London by A. Richter), in which he emulated his American colleague's publication. Dodwell had traveled through Greece in the company of the great classicist Sir William Gell, also an authority on the cultures of ancient Italy, and one can but wonder if Gell might have been Middleton's other companion on several scholarly forays into the Alban hill country.

At least for part of his travels through the Roman countryside, Middleton also enjoyed the company of "a Mr. Philip Giuntotardi, a very distinguished artist in Rome." Filippo Giuntotardi (1768–1831) was a prominent Roman landscapist, engraver, and etcher. As an artist Giuntotardi was influenced by the German painters Josef Anton Koch and Karl Friedrich Schinkel. He was promoted and sponsored by both Schlegel and Frederika Brun, in whose daughter, it has been noted, Middleton had an amorous interest. Later Giuntotardi helped Dodwell with the illustrations to his *Classical and Topographical Tour through*

Lake of Albano. 1st View, from Middleton's Grecian Remains

Continuation of the View from the Summit of Monte Cavo,
from Middleton's Grecian Remains

Greece. It was a small circle! Middleton credited this Italian artist with the execution of five of the drawings for his book as well as with "the original sketches of most of the costume figures which are introduced" into his own compositions. Two of the plates in the *Grecian Remains* show a seated draftsman. Since Giuntotardi provided the figures that Middleton incorporated into his scenes, this draftsman might well be the South Carolinian or possibly his friend Dodwell; however, just as likely, the model could have been an anonymous staffage figure.

Although Middleton played down the importance of the written element in the *Grecian Remains,* what he authored goes beyond a mere commentary to the plates. It is an erudite piece of scholarship, showing an extensive familiarity with both ancient and modern sources. Among the classical writers whom Middleton quoted are Strabo, Pausanius, Status, Vitruvius, Homer, Ovid, Virgil, Pliny, Dionysius, Florus, Apollodorus, and Plutarch. The more modern authorities referenced include Volpi, Justus Ryckius, and Athanasius Kircher. His approach throughout is a model of critical interpretation, for the most part cautious and skeptical. Of the seventeenth-century Jesuit antiquarian Kircher, Middleton, for instance, says: "Many of the conjectures of the good old Kircker are as extraordinary as the plates of his work. The former are the result of neither history nor fable, but a mixture of both; and the latter are neither maps nor pictures." He is, however, careful to point out that "we owe . . . a great deal to him, as he has gathered together in his history of Latium, a great mass of knowledge, as well as of conjecture." All in all, the text that Middleton conceived to accompany his plates was carefully prepared and fully referenced. Clearly, this task required considerable research, and it is easy to imagine Middleton, having interested a publisher, spending long hours among the books of the British Museum Library in London.

The title page of Middleton's *Grecian Remains* bears the publication date of 1812, but the story of how this book was issued is rather complicated. Publication of plates and text evidently was piecemeal. In the copy preserved in the South Caroliniana Library of the University of South Carolina, the paper used up to chapter 4 has watermarks datable to 1805, but thereafter the watermarks come from 1818 to 1823. All the plates have watermarks that are post-1818, with the frontispiece sheet dating from 1823. A copy of the *Grecian Remains* in the British Museum contains some plates with watermarks dated to 1824 and 1825. While some of the plates in the South Caroliniana Library copy have design dates of 1809 and engraving dates of 1811, quite consistent with the official publication date of 1812, other views have an imprint date of 1819. It is thus quite possible that the date of 1812 refers to an official contract or agreement on the publication project; Middleton could have furnished his London publisher with completed works several years earlier or continued work on the project for several years thereafter from South Carolina, where he returned in 1810. The 1818–25 dates are consistent with his return to Europe, where he may have been actively involved in the project. According to one source, a second edition of the *Grecian Remains* appeared in 1820. This could be accurate or it may actually refer to a first bound and complete edition of what had been gradually appearing for over a decade as individual plates and chapters. It is difficult to determine the gap in time between the execution of the twenty-two drawings for the *Grecian Remains* and their initial publication.

Upon the conclusion of his first Italian tour of 1807–9, Middleton was, once more, among the sizable entourage of devotees gathered together, in the spring of 1810, by Madame de Staël at the Castle of Chaumont on the Loire, which the baroness rented from another American acquaintance named James Le Ray. The group assembled not just to savor Staël's brilliance but to bask, yet again, in the beauty of Madame Récamier, who continued to toy not only with young Middleton's affections but also with those of the Russian Baron de Balk, the Germans Schlegel and Casper von Voght, Adrien de Montmorency, and Staël's own son, Auguste de Staël. It was probably during this period that Middleton acquired Pierre-Narcisse Guérin's small replica of Gérard's portrait of Récamier, now at Middleton Place. This was, no doubt, also the occasion at which he wrote his unpublished story "La Confessional," the manuscript of which is conserved in the Southern Historical Collection of the Library of the University of North Carolina at Chapel Hill.

Little is known of Middleton's personal life beyond these few and sketchy details other than the fact that on 11 June 1810, shortly after he had left the charming but frustrating company of Récamier and Staël in the Loire, he married Eliza Augusta Falconnet, the daughter of a Swiss banker resident in Naples named Jean Louis Théodore de Palezieux Falconnet (1760–1825) and an American, Anna Hunter. How Middleton and Miss Falconnet met is unknown, but perhaps the encounter was arranged by Staël, who described a Madame Falconnet in a letter of 1809 as someone who had greatly pleased her in Naples. She, no doubt, was referring to Mrs. Falconnet, who was from a wealthy family in Newport, Rhode Island. The Hunter family records recount that Anna (Johanna) Hunter was taken to England in 1785 by her mother in order for her sister, Catherine, to see a respected Austrian occultist. There she met and married Falconnet, who at the time was in charge of the London branch of his bank.

After their marriage, which took place in Paris, the Middletons set sail for America. They took up residence at Cedar Grove, a large Izard plantation inherited by his mother just across the Ashley River from Middleton Place. How he spent his time is unknown. There is little correspondence from or to him that would indicate his activities except for one 1812 letter in French that discusses the procurement of some indigo for a friend of Monsieur Falconnet. Middleton's mother, Mary Izard Middleton, died in 1814 and passed her inheritance to her second son. This event left him a wealthy man in his own right and enabled him to travel and live how and where he wished. He and Eliza experienced the birth and death from malaria of their only child, a daughter whom they named Anna, in 1815. Whether it was the tragedy of this event and Eliza Middleton's declining health or Izard's intellectual curiosity that helped him to make the decision is unknown, but in 1816 he and Eliza returned to Europe to remain for the rest of their lives. John Izard Middleton sold his properties to his elder brother, Henry, and established a principal residence in Paris. It would seem that he and his wife lived in both France and Italy. Eliza Falconnet Middleton probably never fully recovered from the birth and loss of her child and was eventually looked after by family friends in a quiet country setting away from her husband. An 1820 letter to Septima Sexta Middleton Rutledge, Izard's sister, states that though theirs was a love match, Eliza was separated from her husband and in poor health.

Alicia Hopton Middleton's account describes Eliza as being "the beautiful Miss. Falconet, whose mother was Miss Hunter of Newport, R.I., and her father a Neapolitan." Her impression of Mrs. Middleton's physical appearance undoubtedly was based upon the portrait painted by the eminent Thomas Sully, which she noted as being "one of the few pictures saved from Middleton Place when it was burned. . . ." This same subject was described by Sully in his register of paintings as being a portrait of Mrs. John Izard Middleton, a "half-length, head to the left, with curls, low-necked dress, holds book in hands. Column and curtain in background. Portrait begun July 1st, 1826, finished on July 25th, 1826. Size 27 1/2″ x 36″, canvas. Price, $75.00." The portrait to which the entry refers was actually his second rendering of the attractive Mrs. Middleton. The original was painted while the young couple visited in Philadelphia during the summer and early fall of 1815. Numerous Izards and Manigaults as well as others with Charleston ties lived in the city. Many "occupied a series of very small houses between Ninth and Tenth . . . on Spruce, called commonly from this settlement, Carolina Row," as Joshua Francis Fisher remembered ("Excerpts," p. 137). Middleton was concerned that his wife spend time in the country. While there, they vacationed with the de Kantzows (he was the state minister from Sweden) and visited Mrs. Gabriel Manigault (née Margaret Izard). The Manigault daughter Harriet recorded the event in her diary and noted that "Mrs. Mid. appears to have nearly recovered her health, and looks very beautiful. . . . She was a little reserved at first; but it wore off after awhile, and she was quite charming" (p.117). That charm must have been expertly captured by Sully since the later dated portrait was commissioned from the artist by an admiring Charles Manigault. Unfortunately, the only copy of the portrait on public view that remains today is a much smaller ink-and-wash third version executed at some time by John Izard Middleton.

Alicia Middleton described John Izard Middleton as being "a distinguished artist as well as a diplomat at European courts." How trustworthy this claim of diplomatic service is remains dubious. It is not clear how Middleton really thought of himself, whether as an American living abroad or, despite his father's Revolutionary role, as an Englishman who happened to have been born in America. Certainly, he was mistaken for an Englishman upon occasion. Madame Vigée-Lebrun noted the presence of "un jeune Anglais" among the guests at Coppet in 1807, and it is obvious that she meant Middleton. But America was new and the national distinctions were not as pronounced as they would become; Americans often passed as English on the Continent. It is thus not surprising that the brief entries in both Byron's *Dictionary of Painters and Engravers* and Benezit's *Dictionnaire des peintres, sculpteurs, dessinateurs et graveurs* list Middleton's nationality as English.

Portrait of Eliza Falconnet copied by John Izard Middleton from the original by Thomas Sully. From the permanent collection of the Middleton Place Foundation, Charleston, South Carolina.

A year after the death of Madame de Staël in 1817, Middleton was back in Italy; in fact, it is likely that visits to the peninsula were frequent. His dated watercolors of the *Greek Theater at Taormina with Mt. Etna in the Distance* (1818), now in a private collection, and of *The Temple of Neptune* (Paestum, October 1819), now in the Gibbes Museum of Art in Charleston, indicate that Middleton was wandering about the southern part of the peninsula and Sicily prior to his "second" Roman stay of 1821–23. The Taormina watercolor is thought to be the earliest Sicilian view by an American artist. Middleton's travels into the southern part of Italy may have been occasioned by his wife's Neapolitan connections or the presence of his own family, as well as by his own classical curiosity. Eliza Falconnet Middleton wrote in February 1818 from Capodimonte, outside of Naples, that "Izard has entered so completely into all the gaieties that are going forward, that he cannot stay at home one evening. . . . He is the same in every country, but he certainly passes fewer discontented hours in this, which he is fond of and the climate suits him wonderfully." Eliza Falconnet Middleton's correspondence also reveals vital clues about his travels. In the same letter she related, "He is still bent on performing his journey to Greece, and in April will certainly go there or to Sicily; he has received from England a traveling bed and canteen and although yet he has not made arrangements with a party, he may agree to join one from day to day, as there are several persons going from here soon" (to Mary Hering Middleton, 1 February 1818, Middleton Family Papers). By 27 June, she reports, "Izard is given up Greece, as it is now too late in the season to go there, but set off for Sicily on the 10th." Though the excursion was not without the dangers of bandits and bad weather, Middleton traveled during the summer in order to see Mount Aetna "as the snow prevents travelers from reaching the summit until the end of June." Middleton found the trip exhilarating enough to put off his return by sea from Palermo, instead traveling overland through Tarentium, Lene, and Bari as well as stopping in Messina.

The drawings in *The Roman Remains* series of the Bagni di Lucca, dated 1821, and of what has been tentatively identified here as the harbor of Genoa of 1820 point to the peripatetic nature of Middleton's life and suggest a trip to northern Italy and, perhaps, over the Alps prior to his extended Roman sojourn between 1821 and 1823. It was on this occasion that he did most of the drawings for what he may have intended to be his second volume of views (what in this book has been called *The Roman Remains*). He may have been encouraged to take up this new endeavor by the upcoming issuance of his earlier *Grecian Remains* plates and their accompanying text in a single volume.

Back in Rome in 1821, Middleton may well have met the English literary triumvirate of Keats, Shelley, and Byron. After all, the community of Rome's *Inglesi* (the English), as all of the city's foreign visitors were called, was a tight one. Rembrandt Peale, a member of the great American painting dynasty, was in Rome a few years later, in 1829, and noted the presence in the city of some three hundred foreign artists and scholars. Perhaps Middleton during his stay a few years earlier had made the acquaintance of some of the same figures whom Peale would later encounter. Among the names mentioned by Peale were "those distinguished for their talents in painting, and . . . most esteemed for colouring—English, Russians, French, and Swiss. Mr. Eastlake, Mr. Severn, Mr. Williams, are celebrated for their taste in groups, characteristic of the country—peasants, pilgrims, robbers, beggars, etc." (*Notes on Italy,* pp. 166–67).

Though he undoubtedly felt at home in Rome, one can assume that Middleton, along with the rest of Rome's foreign colony, frequented the celebrated Caffé Greco on the Via Condotti. Opened in the mid eighteenth century, this establishment, more than two hundred years later, is still in operation at its original location. In the years in which Middleton was in Rome, the Caffé Greco hosted most of the writers and artists who visited and resided in the city. Peale was impressed by the locale and those who frequented it:

> After dinner, a neighboring coffee-house, called the Cafe Greco, is thronged with the mixed multitude of the sons of paint. In the cloud of tobacco smoke, it was difficult to distinguish the whiskers, mustachios, and chin tufts of your acquaintance from those of strangers; and the din of voices, that had been reserved all day, made it necessary to bellow into the ear of him who would listen to you. As I found that neither the smoke nor noise were pleasant to my senses, and the increasing din could not be mistaken for conversation, I was always glad to escape after a few minutes' observation of the scene. (*Notes on Italy,* p. 169)

One can but wonder if Middleton sipped coffee with Byron or Keats in the dense atmosphere of the Caffé Greco; he would have just missed the opportunity, however, of exchanging pleasantries with two of England's greatest painters: Sir Thomas Lawrence, who was in Rome from 10 May to 22 December 1819; and J. M. W. Turner, who was in the city from October to December the same year. During his Roman ramblings he may well have encountered his fellow countryman Theodore Dwight, who was in Rome in 1821 and three years later published a journal of his travels accompanied by his own camera obscura–assisted engravings. In Rome, Middleton also may have crossed paths with the young New Englander George Bancroft, who toured the city in 1822 and some years later would achieve fame for his great *History of the United States.* In this period Middleton may even have taken up quarters in the nearby Piazza di Spagna, as did so many *stranieri.* If so, he may have enjoyed the hospitality of the Hotel d'Europe, where Anna Jameson stayed in March of 1822 and where, according to her *Diary of an Ennuyée,* "after nine in the evening a profound stillness reigns," allowing her to "distinguish nothing from my window but the splashing of the

Fountain della Barchetta [Barcaccia]" (p. 283). On the other hand, he could have lodged with equal comfort at the Swiss Hotel, described by his compatriot Theodore Dwight in 1821 as having "very comfortable lodgings" and as being "the principal resort of strangers of all nations" (*A Journal of a Tour in Italy*, pp. 212–13). But Middleton may not have had to stay in a hotel at all; there is good evidence to suggest that his in-laws had a residence in the city, in which case he and his wife would have been staying with them. Another possibility is that, as a man of some means, he may have had his own rooms in the city.

Middleton's prior membership in the celebrated circle of Madame de Staël and his marriage into a Franco-Swiss family would have given him entrée into the French community that included the great Jean Auguste Dominique Ingres, who resided in Rome at the French Academy from 1806 to 1820. His international connections and the "freedom" he enjoyed as an American abroad would also have permitted an association with Italian artists such as the sculptor Antonio Canova (who died on 12 October 1821, while Middleton was at work on his drawings presented here) and the genre painter and illustrator Bartolomeo Pinelli, as well as with the growing contingent of German artists then in Rome. These included Josef Anton Koch, Rudolf and Wilhelm Schadow, Friedrich Overbeck, Franz Pforr, Peter Cornelius, Philipp Veit, and the "Nazarenes," who gathered either at the Villa Malta where Alexander von Humbolt's brother, Wilhelm, was Prussian consul general or at the Convento di San Isadoro where the Bavarians clustered. They all were, of course, *Stammgäste* at the Caffé Greco.

It is further possible that Middleton may have known the famous German classicist Barthold Georg Niebuhr, who lived in Rome as he composed his monumental three-volume *History of Rome*. If Middleton did, indeed, meet Niebuhr, he also would have made the acquaintance of that scholar's young secretary, the brilliant Frans Lieber, who later would immigrate to the United States. In America, Lieber would edit (and largely write) the first edition of the *Encyclopedia Americana*, champion both prison reform and an international code of justice, staunchly uphold the cause of abolitionism, and become an illustrious professor at both South Carolina College (now the University of South Carolina) and Columbia University. Middleton would have had the misfortune, however, of just missing the lovely and erudite Countess of Blessington, who also had known Madame de Staël but who did not arrive in Rome until 1823, when, according to the dating of the drawings, Middleton already had moved northward into France. His departure also prevented another encounter with Madame Récamier, who made her second journey (the first was in 1813–14) to Italy and Rome in November 1823, remaining on the peninsula until April 1825.

Shortly after he executed his second set of Italian drawings (those reproduced here) the *Philadelphia Mercury* had occasion to publish "A Letter from Rome" on 6 August 1823, in which the unnamed correspondent noted that "A Mr. Middleton, from Charleston, America, himself an excellent landscape painter, has purchased in Italy, in a few years, a collection of Pictures which would do honour to the palace of a Prince even in the old world." The contents of that collection and its disposition remain unrecorded. There is no certainty that any of it ended up in America, although perhaps some of the pictures did return following his death. One likely survivor of Middleton's princely collection may be the little gouache-on-ivory copy of Guido Reni's *Beatrice Cenci* now the property of Middleton Place Foundation. Middleton's acquisition of this particular work may have been inspired by Shelley's tragic poem *The Cenci,* which appeared in 1819. Other remnants of his collection may include the 1808 Guérin copy of Gérard's *Madame Récamier* and the Rudolf Schadow sculpture *Wood Nymph.*

In addition to the illustrations for the *Grecian Remains* and the recently recovered drawings for *The Roman Remains,* Middleton's own artistic legacy has had only a limited survival; examples of his paintings and watercolors can be found in private collections and at both the Gibbes Museum of Art in Charleston and at Middleton Place. Alicia Hopton Middleton noted that "some of the watercolors [at Middleton Place] were the work of John Izard Middleton, who was a distinguished artist. . . ." Although many of these may have perished in the Civil War destruction of the estate, two of his large watercolor paintings hang for public viewing at the Middleton Place house: one is entitled *View from My Window at the Hotel Sibella, Tivoli,* dated to 1808; and the other is a splendid panorama of the Ponte Molle and the Tiber River valley (also see Plate 1) as seen from the slopes of Monte Mario. This latter work bears comparison with the later vistas of Thomas Cole and his fellow artists of the Hudson River School. As yet unpublished and little known are an additional album of drawings and watercolors, including many handsome botanical studies executed in South Carolina, and a quantity of Neapolitan drawings, all still preserved at Middleton Place.

John Izard Middleton's obituary published in the *Charleston Courier* on 10 November 1849 noted that he had died "at his house in Paris, where he had been a resident of upwards of 30 years." Little is known of the last thirty years of his life. An entry in the travel journal of Alicia Russell Middleton Gibbes for the year 1835 mentions calling on the elder Middleton in Paris and expresses the opinion that he looks very old. There are undoubtedly sources of information on the life of John Izard Middleton that have not yet been uncovered. He appears to have been a reluctant letter writer since few of his letters exist. Even his wife, Eliza Falconnet Middleton, noted in a letter of 27 June 1818 to Mary Hering Middleton, "He has written to me a few times, for which I am grateful, as he hates to take up a pen" (Middleton Family Papers). His estate was dispersed by his Charleston relatives, and his body was returned to Middleton Place for burial within the family vault, also despoiled in 1865. His wife had predeceased him by several years.

An Appreciation of Middleton Published in 1885

Charles Eliot Norton

Middleton and his accomplishments languished in obscurity until rediscovered by Charles Eliot Norton, who published the following essay in 1885, undoubtedly in commemoration of the hundredth anniversary of the South Carolinian's birth. At the time the article appeared in the first issue of the *American Journal of Archaeology,* Norton occupied a place of preeminence in American scholarship, respected for both his erudition and his breadth of interests.

Norton was born into a New England ministerial family in 1827. After receiving a traditionally classical education, he graduated from Harvard University in 1846 at the age of nineteen. Employed for a time by an importing firm, he traveled extensively in India, the Near East, Egypt, and Europe into the 1850s. His first visit to Rome apparently did not take place until 1855, but it left a decided and lasting impression upon the young aesthete:

> Yes, this is Rome. . . . It is all and far more than I believed it, and yet far less too. I have never been in any place in which Nature seemed to show so kindly, constant, and loving a regard to the works of men, where she does so much to hide their defects, to soften down their harshnesses, and to unite them in one combination of beauty with her own perfect self. (Norton, *Letters,* pp. 143–44)

These Roman impressions lingered with Norton throughout his life, heightening his aesthetic responses and certainly awakening in him a sensitivity to the accomplishments of John Izard Middleton in that American's earlier efforts at archaeological awareness:

Beneath the very pavement of the streets and squares of Rome lie buried treasures of Art. . . . The bosom of the earth has been, and is still, the great storehouse of sculpture. . . . The Roman gardeners, in making their trenches for cabbages or cauliflowers, will still find some long-hidden marble or turn up some broken inscription. Or, if digging be stopped, the rains will do a partial work. . . . Such discoveries as these—worth much to one who comes from a land whose soil is barren in carved stones—will be made by every one who frequents the Campagna. My table is already loaded with bits of marble, pieces of inscriptions, fragments of brick ornament, and parcels of mosaic, that I have picked up in the fields, on my walks during this last month. (Norton, *Notes of Travel*, pp. 227–28)

In 1857, together with James Russell Lowell, Henry Wadsworth Longfellow, and Ralph Waldo Emerson, Norton assisted in founding the *Atlantic Monthly*, and in 1864 he joined with Lowell in establishing the *North American Review*. In 1865 he also helped to found *The Nation*. Between 1869 and 1874 Norton returned to Italy to embark upon an extensive study of Dante, which eventually resulted in his celebrated translation of the poet's *Divine Comedy* in 1892. Back from his researches in Italy, Norton received an appointment as the first professor in art history at Harvard University, a position he held until his retirement in 1898. Among his many and varied publications, the most notable and lasting, in addition to the Dante translation, have been his edited volumes of correspondence from John Ruskin (1904) and Thomas Carlyle (1883–91), as well as his art history monographs, *Historical Studies of Church-Building in the Middle Ages* (1880) and *History of Ancient Art* (1891). Particularly important to his essay on Middleton was Norton's role as the first president of the Archaeological Institute of America; he published his article in the first issue of that organization's journal.

Although Norton may have come across the *Grecian Remains* on his own, it is likely that his attention was called to the volume and its author by Middleton's Charleston relatives. The Middleton family summered in Newport, Rhode Island, where Norton's family had built a summer residence. He met the Middletons in the early 1850s and established a warm relationship with them, visiting their South Carolina plantation in 1855. That trip introduced Norton to the horrors of slavery and also, perhaps, to the antiquarian studies of their expatriate relative.

The First American Classical Archaeologist, by Charles Eliot Norton, as published in the American Journal of Archaeology 1 (1885): 3–9

In the year 1812 a volume in folio, with numerous colored plates, was published in London, with the following title: "Grecian Remains in Italy, a Description of Cyclopian Walls and of Roman Antiquities. With topographical and picturesque Views of Ancient Latium. By J. J. Middleton." In the Introductory Chapter the author says that it is his intention to give an idea of those monuments in Latium which are of a date anterior to Roman greatness. In work of this kind, he says, "The artist is perhaps of more real use than the scholar. I for this reason adopted the plan of making a collection of very accurate drawings. The views, therefore, which are now offered to the public are not meant merely to accompany the text; they are the principal object of this publication. I write, because I have drawn." He adds: "These sketches were executed during the years 1808 and 1809; and it is more than is absolutely necessary to add that the country they are intended to give an idea of was visited in the company of two English gentlemen, then resident at Rome; but I am happy to seize every opportunity of assuring them how much I value their friendship, and how pleasing it is to me to recollect the days I passed with them." This sentence contains in the word "English" the sole indication which the volume affords that the author himself was not an Englishman. The book has an air of good breeding, taste, and learning, which mark its writer as a gentleman, but afford no hint as to his country.

The volume appeared at an unfortunate moment for obtaining the notice it deserved. The last years of the struggle with Napoleon were too full of immediate interest to permit much attention to antiquity. The war between the United States and Great Britain for three years interrupted the literary as well as the political relations between the two countries. Mr. Middleton's book may have attracted the regard of a few scholars and artists; but it disappeared from view before its value was recognized, and before securing for its author the repute which he deserved. His name is not found in Allibone's *Dictionary;* his book is not mentioned by Lowndes, Brunet, or Graesse; C. O. Mueller, Stark and Reinach in their respective Manuals make no reference to the work, or to the writer. A brief and insufficient notice of Mr. Middleton is contained in Appleton's *Cyclopaedia;* but his name has generally been forgotten, and his work has been unknown to those who have followed him in the same field of study. Even if his book had little original value, had become antiquated, and were now superseded, it would still deserve to be rescued from oblivion, as the first contribution made by an American to the knowledge of classical antiquity. But it deserves this for its own sake: the accuracy and excellence of the drawings reproduced in it give it such permanent worth that it may well form the corner-stone of the growing library of American treatises on classical archaeology, while its author's name properly stands at the head of the fast lengthening list of American investigators of the "monuments of former men" in the Old World.

Mr. John Izard Middleton belonged to the well-known South Carolinian family, long distinguished alike for its historic public service and for the hereditary high culture of its leading members. He was the son of the patriot, and signer of the Declaration of Independence, Arthur Middleton, and was born in 1785. He lost his father in infancy, and, like him, received his college education at Cambridge, England. From the University he proceeded to the Continent, and in Italy and France spent the greater part of his life. Endowed by nature with uncommon gifts, which he had cultivated to advantage, he found ready access to good society, and was received on terms of intimacy in circles into which foreigners seldom gained entrance. He sought for no public distinctions, and spent the greater part of his life in elegant, if not indolent, leisure. With his facile powers and varied gifts, with all the graces and accomplishments of culture, it would seem that he needed only ambition to secure the repute for which he did not care. He died in Paris in 1849. His body was brought to America, and buried in the family vaults at Middleton Place, on Ashley River, in South Carolina. The house was burned and the vaults dishonored by the Union troops in 1864[*]; and among the family memorials which were then miserably dispersed or destroyed were some of the beautiful drawings of Mr. Middleton.

It was soon after quitting Cambridge that he went to reside in Italy. The attention of students of antiquity had lately been drawn to the prehistoric walls in Latium by the researches of M. Petit-Radel. To these walls this scholar had given the name of Cyclopean, because they seemed to him to exhibit the same character as those of Tiryns, Mycenae, and other ancient Greek sites, which the Greek writers themselves had attributed to the mythical race of Cyclopes. Observing the methods of construction of these primitive walls, the evidences of comparative antiquity which they afforded, and the sites where they were found, he conceived the idea that they were in truth the work of the Pelasgi, a race which up to this time had appeared scarcely less mythical than the Cyclopes themselves. French scholarship at this time was not at its best, "L'étude de l'Antiquité était alors chez nous en train de renaître," says Sainte-Beuve, speaking of the First Empire. M. Petit-Radel was something of a pedant, and his conclusions were suspected as resting on too narrow a basis of evidence. Published in the "Magasin encyclopédique" in 1804 and subsequent years, they at first met with little acceptance, especially from German archaeologists; and it was not until the subsequent investigations of Dodwell and Gell in Greece and the islands of the Mediterranean had confirmed his views, that the Pelasgic origin of these ancient walls came to be regarded as probable, and that a division of them was established into three or four different orders, according to the shaping and laying of their stones.

Dodwell, who had previously visited Greece, was one of the "English gentlemen" in whose company Mr. Middleton had drawn and studied the Latian walls. He did not fail to note the resemblance between the Cyclopean work of one land and the other; but it was not till 1818 that he published his excellent "Classical and Topographical Tour through Greece," in which he drew attention once more to these oldest remains of European civilization. Had the publication of Mr. Middleton's observations been equally delayed, they might have been as well received and remembered. His book was the first, so far as I am aware, in which the conclusions of M. Petit-Radel were

---

[*] Really 1865. Eds.

supported by fresh evidence and illustrated by accurate drawings. In his opening chapter he says:—

> Pausanias was the first who gave the generic term Cyclopian to the walls of the nature of those we treat of; but I believe no regular system was built upon the observation of their singularity, until about twelve years ago, when Mr. Petit Radel, a member of the National Institute in Paris, published a memoir on the subject; in this tract he terms them "Constructions polygones, irregulières," and endeavors to prove, first, that they have no connection with the "opus incertum" of Vitruvius; and secondly, that they are the remains of monuments built by the Pelasgians.

The first part is very easily established, and is evident to any person who has seen the two modes of construction, as the "opus incertum" is only the embryo of the "opus reticulatum," and differs from the Cyclopian in being composed of small bricks, whereas the Cyclopian walls are built of immense stones, five, ten, fifteen, and occasionally twenty feet long, without any cement, but joined by the nicety of the squaring, and kept together by their own weight. Alberti has mentioned these walls in his Roman Antiquities (B.I.,c.3); and Piranesi, when he speaks of them, calls them erroneously, "opus incertum."

His second theory is scarcely less established, according to my opinion, by the circumstantial evidence of the similarity between these walls and those of many towns in Greece. There is scarcely any doubt of their being of Grecian origin, on account of this similarity, and because those walls are not to be found in any part of the Roman territory, except in that tract of country which Dionysius of Halicarnassus tells us was peopled by Pelasgian colonies.

Albano from the Road to the Lake, from Middleton's Grecian Remains

"The mystery," adds Mr. Middleton, "that envelops this particular branch of the history of arts adds very much to the interest it inspires; . . . the Greeks themselves could have known little more of them" than we, "since they attributed them to the hands of giants."

The third and fourth chapters of Mr. Middleton's book are occupied with a discussion of the original inhabitants of Latium and of the first Latin kings. They are full of the flavor of a fine old-fashioned learning, a little dry with age, but giving evidence of a love for the classics and an acquaintance with them more common among young gentlemen eighty or a hundred years ago than at the present day. In his fifth chapter, when Mr. Middleton sets out from Rome to Albano, the Roman poets are his chosen companions, while the road and the scene derive their chief interest for him from their poetic and historic associations.

Mr. Middleton's course led him along the Appian Way, through Albano, to the Lake of Nemi and its environs, thence to Velletri, and so by Lake Giuliano to Cora. Here the true Cyclopean region begins. Cora, Norba, Segni, Alatri, Ferentino, crowning their steep hills with mighty walls, hardly out of sight one from the other, show how dense the local Pelasgic population must have been of old, how long and terrible were its wars, and how high was the civilization which needed the protection of defenses so elaborate in design, so enormous in scale, and which required such vast and protracted effort, and such immense labor for their construction. At Cora, with the exception of a single square tower, the walls that now remain were raised for the purpose of supporting the hill. At Norba there is an enormous gate, and in general the walls "are very well preserved and are a fine specimen of Cyclopian work." The remains at Segni and at Alatri are of more importance. They are fully described and carefully illustrated by Mr. Middleton; and it seems worth while to quote a portion of his account of them to show the character of his archaeological observations.

> The hill on which Segni is situated is very steep, and we were nearly two hours ascending its barren sides. . . . The modern town of Segni lies enclosed within the ancient walls, but does not occupy half the space of the ancient city. As usual, in the places where Cyclopian remains are found, the site cannot be better adapted for defense; as, with the exception of the gate by which you enter modern Segni, the other entrances were placed immediately on the edge of the steep sides of the mountain. . . . The walls are of the highest antiquity. Of the first style of the Cyclopian, which is formed of rude masses of stone piled up in order to form a wall, I have seen nowhere such remains, except a portion of a wall at Cora, and another at Palestrina. . . . The walls form an enclosure of upwards of two miles in circumference. We found eight ancient gates, of which four had their architraves perfect. We dug to the bases of these four, and found that the earth had in general encroached from two to three feet. . . . The first and largest gate, vulgarly called Porta Saracena, . . . is about ten feet high and eight feet wide, and is composed of five enormous blocks,—two upright, two inclining to an angle of about forty degrees, while the fifth forms the architrave, which appears carelessly thrown across. The second, third, and fourth gates are smaller, with no striking peculiarities. We come now to a small pointed gate,

*Exterior of the Great Cyclopian Gate at Norba,
from Middleton's Grecian Remains*

*Exterior of the Great Cyclopian Gate of the Ancient Citadel of Alatri,
from Middleton's Grecian Remains*

placed in a wall which serves to prop the earth. The point at the top is formed, on one side by a stone which makes, with the upright, an obtuse angle, and on the other by a curve as regularly formed as that of the Gothic-pointed arch. The entrance in this gate, as in several others, is not immediately straight, but sideways, so that, of the stones which form the corners, one has an acute and the other an obtuse angle.

Mr. Middleton, after describing the remaining gates, speaks of the ancient substruction of the modern church and makes an instructive observation:

I observed near this church, as in several other places in Segni where the Cyclopian work had been in part demolished, a peculiarity which may throw some light upon the mode of construction of these remote nations whenever they wished to attain any additional strength or solidity. On the interior surface of the stones, which have been left uncovered by the demolition of the upper part of the wall, are oblong holes cut in the block, some about eight or ten inches long, an inch wide, and from two or three deep. By conceiving that the upper stone, which fitted upon these, was hollowed in the same manner, it would allow space for the introduction of a piece of wood or iron, about ten inches long, by four or six broad; and this, tightly incased within the wall, prevented the stones from being removed out of their place by any external injury.

Proceeding now to Alatri,—

As you enter the gate of San Pietro, a peculiarity is observable which is afforded by none of the above-mentioned towns. On the exterior and interior walls, adjacent to the gate, are two bassi rilievi,[1] which are almost defaced by time; but which, after having been accurately examined, both on the spot and through the means of a cast of a mould taken from one of them, are determined by the antiquaries to be the "Custos furum atque avium, cum falce saligna."— *Georg.* IV. 110.

. . . The citadel on the side where this gate is situated is defended by a very high bastion, which supports the platform of the ancient level, and the gate is opened in this bastion. The whole of this bastion, which extends in equal dimensions round the greatest part of the citadel, is formed of immense polygonal blocks; and the stone, which forms the architrave of the gate, is nearly fifteen feet and a half in length, seven feet broad, and seven feet thick. The thickness of the wall, at the place you enter by this gate, is forty-three feet.

On the opposite side of the citadel is a small gate, upon the architrave of which is a carving of one of those "satyrica signa," which till a late period the Romans were accustomed to represent in similar places "contra invidentium effascinationes." "The delicacy of one of the bishops of Alatri induced him to deface this very curious monument of antiquity, and it is now precisely in the state in which I have represented it." A photograph by Mr. Stillman, of this gate, affords evidence of the extraordinary accuracy of Mr. Middleton's drawing.

---

[1]Mr. Middleton gives a plate representing the gate, with these reliefs. Its perfect accuracy is confirmed by a recent photograph taken by Mr. W. J. Stillman, whose studies of Pelasgic walls have probably been wider and more thorough than those of any other living archaeologist.

Every block of the gate and the adjoining wall appear in the engraving not less exactly than in the photograph itself; and the comparison of these two representations, as well as of others where Mr. Stillman has taken the same view, establishes the entire trustworthiness of Mr. Middleton's plates.[2]

With a description of the rock-cut tombs of Valmontone, of the remains at Palestrina, and of the objects of interest on the way between this latter town and Rome, Mr. Middleton concludes his work.

Twenty-two years after the publication of his volume, some of the same drawings which had been reproduced in it were once more engraved, in an inferior style, for the well-known posthumous work of Mr. Dodwell, on the *Cyclopian, or Pelasgic, Remains in Greece and Italy*.[3] The book contains no reference to the young American who had been the companion of its author in the study of Latian antiquities, and whose own book had failed to secure the attention it deserved.[*]

---

* Middleton, Petit-Radel, and, later, Norton were wrong in supposing the so-called Cyclopean or Pelasgic walls of the hill towns south of Rome to be of extreme antiquity. It has been substantiated by archaeological evidence that they are of Roman republican origin, constructed primarily to bulwark the Roman territorial advance. That many a nineteenth-century scholar was mistaken about their origins is not surprising, however, since they do, at least superficially, resemble the walls of Mycenaean communities. In spite of the error in dating, Middleton's drawings have distinct value today, documenting as they do the various states of preservation and revealing once again the fascination with which he and his contemporaries regarded the countryside traces of the past. They also are a clear testimony that the artist was quite right in holding his visual record to be of more lasting value than his verbal. Eds.

---

[2] This exactness was attained by him by means of the camera obscura. "The greater part of my outlines," he says, "indeed, I may say all the distances and those parts of the picture which require the accuracy of the antiquary more than the grace of the artist," are secured by the mechanical process. "I afterwards retouched them on the spot, and gave that grace of detail which it was impossible to attain while the paper was under the lens." The engravings were colored by hand to resemble the original drawings.

[3] The full title of this work is, *"Views and Descriptions of the Cyclopian, or Pelasgic, Remains in Greece and Italy; with constructions of a later period: from drawings by the late Edward Dodwell, Esq., F.S.A., London, 1834. 131 plates and 34 pages of letter-press, folio."*

The Romance of Rome

The City and Its Visitors in the Early Nineteenth Century

Charles R. Mack

According to tradition, Rome was founded by the divine twins Romulus and Remus on 21 April 753 B.C. Disregarding the specifics of this legend, the general dating of the first Roman settlement is attested to rather well in the archaeological record. The course of Rome's rise to urban grandeur and imperial dominion is one of those mysteries of history. By the beginning of the second century A.D., Roman might held sway from the highlands of Scotland to the sands of the Sahara and from the further Iberian coast to the Persian Gulf. The city could boast a population in excess of two million, a density extraordinary for the day. With the collapse of the empire in the fifth century, Rome declined as well. Sacked and resacked by barbarian pillagers, the city was preserved by the spiritual force that had struggled against her secular authority. As the eventual seat of the papacy, Rome achieved a new position of leadership, but the breakup of Roman civilization brought a great reduction in the city's population and urban extent. At one point Rome's medieval inhabitants numbered as few as twenty thousand, clustered into an area within the bend of the Tiber across from the ancient Castel Sant'Angelo or scattered around the numerous pilgrimage churches and basilicas. Between these pockets of population, enclosed within the decaying Aurelian walls of the late third century, lay vineyards, olive groves, pasturage for sheep and cows, and bramble-covered ruins.

Rome began its reawakening with the rebirth of culture and art that motivated the Italian Renaissance. From the middle of the fifteenth century, a reinvigorated papacy set about rebuilding a physical splendor in the city that would complement the spiritual position of the Church. The glory of the new Saint Peter's Basilica and the Vatican Palace as well as the renewal of urban development during the sixteenth and seventeenth centuries marked Rome's second coming.

The Rome that Middleton drew in the early 1820s was between transitions. The winds of change that the French Revolution had blown across Europe in the final decade of the previous century had swept away much of the status quo of papal Rome. The city was occupied by a French army in 1798, when a new and secular Roman republic was proclaimed, forcing Pope Pius VI into exile in France, where he died in 1799. In 1800, having acceded to the stipulations of the infant republic, the newly elected Pope Pius VII returned, only to vacate Rome once again when the imperial troops of the emperor Napoleon reoccupied the city in 1810. At this point Rome was proclaimed the second city of the empire by the French Senate, and a year later Napoleon's infant son was decreed king of Rome. The French remained in Rome until the collapse of their empire in 1815. The Congress of Vienna divided the Italian peninsula among the European powers, with most of the north going to Austria (except Genoa, which went to the king of Savoy and Sardinia, Victor Emmanuel) and the south to the Bourbon family. The Papal States were restored, and Pope Pius VII came back to Rome once more in temporal power, a power administered with a general benevolence and even some progressiveness.

The following passage by the English traveler Mariana Starke conveys much of the atmosphere found in Rome in the 1820s:

A View of Rome with the Alban Hills beyond from the Monte Mario, from Middleton's Grecian Remains

Modern Rome is not seventeen Roman miles in circumference; and contains, Suburbs inclusive, scarce one hundred and fifty thousand inhabitants: but reduced as this ancient Mistress of the world now is, in size and population, . . . still the matchless [beauty of her artworks] entitle[s] her to be called the most magnificent City of Europe, and the unrivalled Mistress of the Arts!—Some of her streets, however are ill paved and dirty; while ruins of immense edifices, which continually present themselves to view, give an impression of melancholy to every thinking spectator. The society of Rome is excellent; and the circumstance of every man, whether foreigner or native, being permitted to live as he pleases, without exciting wonder, contributes essentially to general comfort. At Rome, too, every person may find amusement: for whether it be our wish to dive deep into classical knowledge, whether arts and sciences be our pursuit, or whether we merely seek for new ideas or new objects, the end cannot fail to be obtained in this most interesting of Cities, where every stone is an historian:—and though Rome has, in some respects, suffered from her late Rulers, the French, she is, generally speaking, obliged to them; as they removed the earth with which time had buried part of the Colosseum; disencumbered the Temple of Vesta from the plaster-walls which destroyed its beauty; excavated the Forum of Trajan, the Baths of Titus, and the lower parts of the Temples of Fortune, and Jupiter Tonans; removed from the foundations of the Arches of Septimius Severus and Constantine the Rubbish by which they were in some measure concealed; and cleared away from the Temple of Peace [actually the Basilica Nova] an immense collection of earth, which entombed nearly one third of its remains. (Starke, *Travels in Europe*, p. 119)

Culturally and physically Rome was experiencing another resurrection, although her political and social rebirth was still some years distant. Despite a general papal tolerance, the threat of repression was always there. On 24 March 1824, for instance, Pius VII's less tolerant successor, Pope Leo XII, fearing the subversive mingling of politically progressive foreigners with his citizenry, ordered the closure of that popular gathering place, the Caffé Greco. Not all of those touring Rome and Italy were astute enough to mark the coming popular upheaval. One might suppose, however, that Middleton, the child of the first modern democracy and the son of a "Signer," held views similar to those of the Baltimorean James Sloan, who, traveling through Italy in 1816–17, noted that:

No country, perhaps, has suffered more than Italy, from the oppression of overgrown land-holders, and the imbecility inherent in the present governments, helps to nourish and perpetuate this abuse. Here tenures of landed property are upon the worst footing. This is the reason, why vast tracts of her soil lie waste and uncultivated; this is the cause of the indigence, in general, of her peasantry, and the source of that frightful poverty, which exists in a country enjoying the kindest influences of Heaven. (Sloan, *Rambles*, p. 364)

Rome, nevertheless, had entered into a three-decade-long period of relative tranquillity that lasted until 1848 and a new storm of revolutionary agitation. Yet beneath the calm surface, currents of change were at work. Sloan's perceptive observations of the Italian political scene enjoyed a peculiarly American perspective:

I have already noticed the insatiable curiosity, which exists in Italy, relative to the government of the United States. The idea of an extensive country, flourishing and prosperous, to an eminent degree, in which hereditary monarchy, and an hereditary nobility are unknown, possessed peculiar attractions for a people, whom a lively sensibility to the oppressions, and a more enlightened view of the theoretical evils of regal and aristocratik institutions, were awakening to the charms of liberty. . . . Hereditary monarchy and hereditary nobility depend upon illusions, which the freedom of thinking of the eighteenth century has contributed, in great measure, to dispel. The American revolution and the subsequent events in Europe, combined with the general diffusion of knowledge, have enlightened on this subject the mass of mankind, throughout the civilized world. (Sloan, *Rambles,* pp. 366–67)

With the revolutionary wave that swept much of Europe in 1848 came the resurgence of nationalism on the Italian peninsula. This was the period of the great Italian statesmen Giuseppe Mazzini and Count Camillo Cavour and the patriotic generalship of Italy's George Washington, Giuseppe Garibaldi. The great struggle of the *Risorgimento* to free Italy from foreign rule saw another flight of the papacy from Rome and the brief establishment of a new Roman republic. French troops, pledged to defend papal interests, laid siege to the city in 1849. The republican defenders, led by Garibaldi's brigade of "redshirts," put up a brave resistance but eventually were forced to evacuate the city. By 1861 the rest of Italy had been united into a kingdom under Victor Emmanuel of Savoy; however, it was not until 1870, after the withdrawal of the French occupation forces to take part in the Franco-Prussian War, that Rome became part of unified Italy. In 1871 parliament and the government offices were moved from Florence to Rome, beginning the city's evolution into the capital of the fully emergent nation.

Although the political changes for Rome since Middleton's day have been profound, the city's physical transformation has been even greater. From an estimated population of some 150,000 circa 1820, the city has swelled to more than 3 million, more than regaining its ancient size from the days of the Roman emperor Trajan. When Middleton was touring the city, sketchbook and camera obscura in hand, Rome's urban development had not yet reached beyond the ancient boundaries of the city's third-century circuit of walls. In fact, much of the interior of the city was still given over to fields and pasturage, her hallowed pilgrimage churches linked together by winding dirt roadways. Beyond the Capitoline Hill, for all practical purposes, the countryside began, and no suburbs intruded into the Campagna landscape outside the Aurelian walls. Rome was then, perhaps even more than nowadays, a city of tremendous contrast. The romance of discovery abounded: narrow *vicoli* suddenly opened into broad piazze; the squalor of butchershops and fishmongers' stalls flanked the facades of great baroque churches; and brick-faced concrete vaults of noble ruins erupted out of briar-encrusted hillsides. For the tourist, Rome was a place for both scholarship and reverie.

Yet, during Middleton's day the bucolic tranquillity of papal Rome was starting to undergo considerable change, physical transformations that would match the city's growth in population and altered political circumstance. Archaeological explorations, such as those noted earlier in Mariana Starke's account, at first sporadic and later more scientifically methodical, were delving into the mysteries of the ancient Forum and the Coliseum, and in 1821 the architect Giuseppe Valadier totally reconstructed the Arch of Titus. New attempts at an urban systemization of the city also were being made. Valadier already had completed his major work of landscape architecture on the Pincian Hill (1810–18), which today communicates with Rome's other great public park within the grounds of the Villa Borghese. At the behest of Pope Pius VII, the same architect laid out (1816–20) a formalized arrangement for the Piazza del Popolo through which visitors arriving from the north entered Rome. These projects would have certainly attracted Middleton's attention upon his return to Rome in 1821.

Since 1870 extraordinary and sometimes unfortunate efforts at urban renewal have taken place in Rome, dictated most recently by the demands of the city's enormous flow of traffic. Much of today's Rome would be unrecognizable to Middleton. Medieval and picturesque quarters of the city have been demolished and replaced by blocks of high-rise tenements. New thoroughfares now cut through the city in fruitless attempts to relieve traffic congestion. The Via Nazionale, the Corso Vittorio Emanuele II, the Piazza dell'Esedra, the massive railroad station, enormous government buildings necessary to the administration of the Italian state—these and countless other constructions separate late-twentieth-century Rome from the Rome that Middleton knew. Fifteen bridges have been added to the original five spanning the Tiber, and its banks have been rebuilt, following the Parisian model, resulting in the demolition of the old Port of Rome and the creation of broad boulevards paralleling the course of the river. Visitors to Rome remark, with varying reactions, on the King Victor Emmanuel Monument (nicknamed "The Wedding Cake"), an architectural giant that dominates the Piazza Venezia and dwarfs the nearby buildings of the Capitoline Hill. Two of fascism's most destructive contributions to the ancient fabric of the city have taken the form of processional avenues: the secular Viale Imperiale leading to the Coliseum; and its liturgical counterpart, the Via della Concilazione advancing to Saint Peter's.

Thankfully, World War II touched Rome but little; however, in the last half of this century much continues to be done to dismantle and rebuild. After years of fitful construction, Rome's subway system is now a viable part of her communication network. Hosting the games of the 1960 Olympics occasioned accelerated urban change as well. Of course, as all the changes have been taking place within the inner city, the growth beyond the walls has more than kept pace. The enormous residential and commercial impact of the city's southern subdivision, centered about the old Fascist Exposition

Center (EUR), is but one prime example of Rome's continued urban sprawl. Despite the many exciting archaeological revelations, the sense of Rome's historical continuity may not be as clearly discerned today as it was during John Izard Middleton's visits.

All roads seem always to have led to Rome, and along them have journeyed multifarious travelers who have sought in the city various favors and inspirations. In medieval times princes, prelates, and pilgrims made the journey; they were joined in the Renaissance by the intellectually and artistically curious. Still later Rome became a principal destination for those making "the grand tour" of the Continent, hoping thereby to broaden their knowledge and to return to their homes with an absorbed cultural understanding. No aspiring Frenchman, German, Scandinavian, or Englishman (or eventually his American cousin) could have considered himself truly educated without having made the Italian tour. The enthusiasm with which the visitor anticipated his arrival in Rome is clearly announced by the young Goethe in a journal entry written at Civita Castellana on 28 October 1786: "Well then, tomorrow evening Rome! Even now I can hardly believe it. When this wish has been fulfilled, what shall I wish for next." His destination reached, Goethe still seemed in awe when he noted three days later: "Even to myself, I hardly dared admit where I was going and all the way I was still afraid I might be dreaming; it was not till I had passed through the Porta del Popolo that I was certain it was true, that I really was in Rome" (Goethe, *Italian Journey,*). The tourist industry that still does much to sustain the Italian economy had been born, giving legitimacy to the statement that, indeed, all roads still lead to Rome.

There is perhaps no other city about which so much has been written or which has so often been depicted. Rome and its monuments have fascinated artists since the days when Brunelleschi and Donatello traveled from Florence to labor among the ruins, carefully measuring the architectural and sculptural fragments that they would use to help create the Renaissance. A half century later the great humanist scholar Leone Battista Alberti prepared a cartographic record of the city. Still later Rome's numerous sculptures and ruins were being routinely featured in the copybooks of Renaissance masters such as Domenico Ghirlandaio and Giuliano da Sangallo. The most famous of those who devoted great effort to recording and defining the antiquity of the city was Raphael, who did so at the behest of Pope Leo X. Rome was often described and depicted by the foreign traveler as well. In the early years of the sixteenth century the Dutchman Maarten van Heemskerck was among the most celebrated of those who avidly drew the ancient and modern monuments of the papal city. In the next century came the Dutch "Romanists," among them Nicolaes Bercham, Jan Asselijn, and Jan Both, who specialized in romanticized views of the Campagna outside

Rome, and the great French landscapist Claude Lorrain. These artists established a tradition that combined classical rendition with nostalgic fantasy, a genre kept alive throughout the eighteenth century by foreigners such as Hubert Robert and Alexander Cozens, and by the homegrown talent of Giovanni Pannini, Giuseppe Vasi, and Giambattista Piranesi. The general image of Rome and its region that the artists carried away on drawing pads and canvases was a romantic one in which the ruins became even grander and loomed larger than life. At the beginning of the nineteenth century, Madame de Staël neatly summed up the foreigner's attitude about Rome and its historic region:

> In fact, it is not so much the city [of Rome] I loved as a kind of musical, poetic, picturesque, aerial way of life that has opened up to me a new sphere of ideas and sensations—those monuments, those memories, this beautiful sky—the barren countryside surrounding Rome, which is not arid but which seems to mourn its former owners. . . . What attracts me in this city is a mystery that does not reveal itself on first acquaintance, a sensation of the South that is completely unknown to those who have not been there, a certain sympathy between nature and man that cannot be imagined anywhere else—and a noble and calm image of death in the tombs and the traces of great men.
>
> (Letter of 1807 quoted in Herold, *Mistress to an Age,* pp. 309–10)

As the new century advanced, published travel journals and touristic guides were becoming an established literary genre. The appearance of those in the English language accelerated once the Napoleonic Wars were at an end and the Continent reopened to cross-channel tourism; most likely Middleton had access to the most current and popular of them. Among these were J. Salmon's *An Historical Description of Ancient and Modern Rome,* which was published in 1800; Joseph Forsyth's *Remarks on Antiquities* of 1813; the Reverend John Eustace's *A Classical Tour through Italy,* which first appeared in 1815; and the *Recollections Abroad* of Richard Colt Hoare, which came out two years later although written between 1785 and 1787. Of more recent date was the illustrated volume by James Hakewell titled *A Picturesque Tour of Italy,* published in 1820. These would have formed a basic compendium for Middleton's own explorations, supplemented by the recently published guides of W. A. Cadell, Charlotte Eaton, and Mariana Starke. Antonio Nibby's study of the Roman Forum had recently been issued and most certainly would have attracted the archaeologically minded Middleton, as would have the first volumes of Niebuhr's great *History of Rome* and Mariano Vasi's *A New Picture of Rome and its Environs.* He also would have enjoyed the written impressions of his American forerunners Joseph Sansom, James Sloan, and Matthias Bruen.

Yet Middleton's inquisitive character evidently forced him to delve deeper. His commentary to the *Grecian Remains* makes clear his thorough knowledge of a vast array of classical authors as well as the rather obscure writings of seventeenth-century "authorities" and latter classicists. There can be no doubt that Middleton embarked upon his scholarly and pictorial investigations well armed with a broad selection of critical studies and a thorough literary knowledge of the Roman region.

Middleton, no doubt, shared the romantic emotions of Madame de Staël as well as the archaeological curiosity of the classical scholar, but he also would have brought with him an American viewpoint, engendered by the sense of contrast he would have found between his New World origins and his present situation within the Old World establishment. That distinctly American interpretation is echoed thirty years later in the comments of James Russell Lowell, who noted that Italy

> was classic ground, and this not so much by its association with great events as with great men . . . [having] a magnetic virtue quite peculiar to her, which compels alike steel and straw, finding something in men of the most diverse temperaments by which to draw them to herself. . . . But to the American, especially if he be of an imaginative temper, Italy has a deeper charm. She gives him cheaply what gold cannot buy for him at home, a Past at once legendary and authentic, and in which he has an equal claim with every other foreigner. In England he is a poor relation whose right in the entail of home traditions has been docked by revolution; of France his notions are purely English . . . but Rome is the mother country of every boy who has devoured Plutarch or taken his daily doses of Florus. Italy gives us antiquity with good roads, cheap living, and, above all, a sense of freedom from responsibility. . . . Coming from a country where everything seems shifting like a quicksand, where men shed their homes as snakes their skins . . . the sense of permanence, unchangeableness, and repose which Italy gives us is delightful. (Lowell, *Fireside Travels,* pp. 148–50)

Despite all the many and wrenching changes that have occurred in the Italian scene, these are sentiments with which the modern American visitor might still agree, and they serve to connect John Izard Middleton's reverential vision of Italy with what we observe today.

Rome as Seen by Its Nineteenth-Century Visitors

1817–18

> Rome!—Yes, we are actually in Rome, at least I believe so, for as yet I can scarcely feel sure of the fact; and, as in restless impatience we pace up and down the room, and, looking round, see that it is like any other room, we continually ask each other in astonishment, if we are indeed in Rome, if we shall really to-morrow see the Coliseum, the Forum, and St. Peter's, or if, after all, it is only a dream?

> Charlotte Eaton,
> *Rome in the Nineteenth Century,* I, p. 92.

1818

> With Rome, I find every day more reason to be contented; and if I were condemned to live in Europe, I am sure this is the place I should choose

for my exile beyond any other I have yet seen. Nature here is so beautiful, as soon as you leave the immediate environs and go a little way among the hills, that it seems as if the works of man were hardly necessary for his happiness,—and yet where has man done so much? Antiquity has left such traces of splendor and magnificence that Rome might be well content with ruins alone,—and yet the modern city has more fine buildings than all the rest of the world beside. . . . But these are not all the attractions of Rome, for they bring here a deputation from the elegant and refined class from every nation in Europe, who, when united, form a society such as no other capital can boast. . . .

George Ticknor,
Life, Letters, and Journals, pp. 172–73.

1818–19

No other city is so calculated to raise and keep up the finer feelings of the mind; no other can present to us, so forcibly and so tangibly, the histories which we have read with so much delight, or make us sympathise so strongly with catastrophes of patriots and heroes.

Edward Burton,
A Description of the Antiquities and Other Curiosities of Rome, I, p. 17.

1819

Of Rome I can say nothing to you, but express fruitless wishes for your being here, and feelings of increased astonishment and admiration and AFFECTION for it, that its greatness and beauty demand from us. The remains of its earlier grandeur, are many of them on so vast a scale, and convey such an idea of power, and habitual notions of the magnificent and great, that they seem less exertions of men as they now are, than the equal and ordinary productions of another scale of being; their very pavement seems that of a race of giants, whilst the exceeding beauty of the hues and tints, and corresponding harmony of the sky, give a charm to the whole effect that divests it of every gloomy or depressing feeling, and fixes the mind in a state of the purest admiration that it is possible for it to enjoy. . . .

Sir Thomas Lawrence, quoted in D. E. Williams,
The Life and Correspondence of Sir Thomas Lawrence, II, pp. 157–58.

1828

I have been so much delighted with Rome, that I have extended my residence in Italy much beyond my original intention. There is so much in this city to delay the stranger—the villages in the environs are so beautiful—and there is such a quiet and stillness about everything, that were it in my power I should be induced to remain the whole year round. You can imagine nothing equal to the ruins of Rome. The Foro Romano and the Coloseum are beyond all I had ever fancied them:—and the ruined temples—the mausoleums—and the old mouldering acqueducts which are scattered in every direction over the immense plain which surrounds the city—give you an idea of the ancient grandeur of the

Romans, and produce in your mind ideas, which cannot easily be defined, nor communicated.

Henry Wadsworth Longfellow,
Letters of Henry Wadsworth Longfellow, I, p. 261.

1841–44

Nothing can be found so like Paradise as Italy . . . in sober truth, no other country contains a tenth part of its advantages for the painter. . . . Seven months residence at Rome convinces me that the decision of the learned in art is correct—that Rome stands without a competitor as furnishing the materials for a painter . . . the gods be praised that my home is here.

James De Veaux, quoted in Robert Gibbes,
A Memoir of James De Veaux, of Charleston, pp. 164–65, 138–39.

1846

There is nothing in the world like Rome. Here was picturesque material on every side in superabundance. And here were American friends and artists. The famous places to be seen, St. Peter's, the Coliseum, and other celebrated ruins, the Vatican, the Capitoline and other galleries, the villas outside the walls, the Carnival,—the endless sights to be seen,—these in themselves were enough to occupy us from day to day. But there were open-air pictures waiting to be painted everywhere around us, and on the wonderful Campagna, so that there was a perpetual stimulus to draw and paint. The climate was so mild that working out of doors was usually practicable.

Christopher Pearse Cranch, quoted in Leonora Cranch Scott,
The Life and Letters of Christopher Pearse Cranch, pp. 104–5.

1856

For one, I now really live in Rome, and I begin to see and feel the real Rome. She reveals herself day by day; she tells me some of her life. Now I never go out to see a sight, but I walk every day; and here I cannot miss of some object of consummate interest to end a walk. . . . As one becomes familiar, Ancient and Modern Rome, at first so painfully and discordantly jumbled together, are drawn apart to the mental vision. One sees where objects and limits anciently were; the superstructures vanish, and you recognize the local habitations of so many thoughts. When this begins to happen, one feels first truly at ease in Rome. Then the old kings, the consuls and tribunes, the emperors, drunk with blood and gold, the warriors of eagle sight and remorseless beak, return for us, and the togated procession finds room to sweep across the scene; the seven hills tower, the innumberable temples glitter, and the Via Sacra swarms with triumphal life once more. Ah! how joyful to see once more *this* Rome, instead of the pitiful, peddling, Anglicized Rome, first viewed in unutterable dismay from the *coupe* of the vettura,—a Rome all full of taverns, lodging-houses, cheating chambermaids, vilest *valets de place,* and fleas!

Margaret Fuller, Countess Ossoli,
At Home and Abroad, p. 259.

1867

But the surest way to stop writing about Rome is to stop. I wished to write a real "guide-book" chapter on this fascinating city, but I could not do it, because I have felt all the time like a boy in a candy shop—there was everything to choose from and yet no choice.

Mark Twain,
Innocents Abroad, II, p. 12.

The Roman Remains

Middleton's Unpublished Volume Considered

Charles R. Mack and Lynn Robertson

John Izard Middleton's *Grecian Remains* was but the second book of Italian impressions to have been written by an American, following by seven years the publication of Joseph Sansom's *Letters from Europe*. As such it signaled a growing refamiliarization of Americans with their cultural heritage. Since Middleton's book was both academic and antiquarian in nature, it also marked the beginnings of America's venture into the world of erudite scholarship. The *Grecian Remains,* however, as Norton was careful to point out in his essay, unfortunately appeared at a most inopportune moment and languished for many years in virtual obscurity.

The *Grecian Remains* was essentially rediscovered by Norton, undoubtedly through his personal association with members of Middleton's family, and whatever appreciation it may have found in the last century was largely due to Norton's essay. But by the time Norton called attention to the volume, the popularity of photographs had devalued the worth of the sort of visual field survey that Middleton had carried out almost eight decades earlier. Even Norton had stressed the significance of Middleton's drawings by comparing their accuracy with that of William Stillman's photographs. Then, too, in the light of increasingly scientific archaeological methodologies, the exploratory foraging of Middleton even seemed rather romantic. Today copies of the *Grecian Remains* are to be found in the rarefied surroundings of the special collections divisions of a few older academic libraries, but it and the additional series of forty-nine accurately rendered visualizations published here have achieved a new importance. They not only show what was there, they are invaluable as a part of history and as a testimony to the classical devotion and burgeoning systematic study of antiquity initiated by Middleton's generation. They are fundamental to an understanding of the birth of modern archaeology.

Middleton's accurate renderings and systematic inquiry parallel the growth of archaeology as a science increasingly practiced throughout Italy and, in particular, Rome. With the French occupation of the city at the end of the eighteenth century had come the wholesale removal of antiquities and architectural elements. A strong outcry from French and other intellectuals went against the conquering government's policy of plunder. Public opinion and the determination of Pope Pius VII, elected in 1800, to protect the holy city led to the establishment of the first state agencies charged with the protection of artistic and architectural heritage and a cessation in private collecting. Carlo Fea was given the title of commissioner of antiquities and the responsibility for oversight of ancient churches, monuments, and public buildings, including the approval of archaeological investigations. A number of official excavations were undertaken during the first quarter of the nineteenth century. With Rome's designation as the second capital of the empire, increased financial and government support supplemented archaeological projects. By the time of Middleton's sojourn in the city, urban excavations were proliferating, but work was progressing at a far more professional level than in earlier centuries. Archaeologists such as Antonio Nibby, director of the excavations in the Roman Forum and elsewhere, used medieval texts to help identify sites correctly. Educated amateurs were given permission by the papal offices to conduct their own supervised excavations. Throughout the city there was a constant sound of pickaxes. The Roman Academy, founded in 1810, worked to bring together archaeologists, artists, and amateur scholars from around the world to study the contributions of the Roman world. The first professional archaeological association was founded in 1829 as the Institute of Archaeological Correspondence, dedicated to recording worldwide excavations and establishing new methods.

The artistic recordings of these activities were an important part of the search for ancient civilization. Artists had been recording antiquities for generations, but Middleton's work was part of a new and visually accurate view. The great Piranesi, through whom the wonders of Rome had become widely known, had taken much artistic license with what he depicted in his printed *veduti*, aggrandizing scale and shifting features about to suit his concept of compositional correctness. Yet his maps of Rome reflect a deep interest in recording the remains of Roman civilization. The next generation of classical scholars challenged this sort of editorializing. A few years before Middleton traveled to Italy, Joseph Forsyth had written: "That rage for embellishing, which is implanted in every artist, has thrown so much composition into the engraved views of Rome, has so exaggerated its ruins and architecture, or so expanded the space in which they stand, that a stranger, arriving here with the expectations raised by those prints, will be infallibly disappointed" (Forsyth, *Remarks on Antiquities,* p. 123).

Ancient Tomb in the Garden at Palazzola,
from Middleton's Grecian Remains

Nymphaeum on the Borders of the Lake of Albano,
from Middleton's Grecian Remains

Middleton's eye for reality and his passion for archaeological accuracy rejected such approaches. In its use of a restrained classicism, Middleton's method of draftsmanship was stylistically similar to that practiced in England from the mid eighteenth century. It was the manner in which he most certainly had been instructed. By the end of the eighteenth century, the preference for idealized classical allusion had given way to a more "authentic" treatment of antiquity. This artistic change in style complemented the shift toward an approach to antiquity that marked the "Age of the Encyclopedia" and then the "Age of Winkelmann." The literary romance of an earlier baroque vision was replaced by a drive to authenticate, document, and categorize the heritage of the classical past. Accuracy became a virtue. As Duncan Bull has noted, "Topography, and the topographical style, in that it partook of the preoccupations of archaeology, could become more acceptable as art. Artists could express their enthusiasm for the sites of antiquity by recording them with accuracy and with a minimum of embellishment" (Bull, *Classic Ground,* p. 5).

There is no evidence to indicate who Middleton's drawing instructor might have been, although his manner does show some connection to that of Francis Towne (circa 1740–1816), whose own best works were drawings and watercolors of the Roman region. Towne, however, worked up his field sketches in the studio and is not known to have employed the camera obscura as a visual aid. Technically, some similarity also can be found between Middleton's loose use of loops and curls and that employed by Joseph Farington (1747–1821), one of the most socially prominent English artists of the day.

The illustrations for Middleton's *Grecian Remains* were rendered in hand-colored aquatint, and one might reasonably assume that if the drawings included in *The Roman Remains* originally had been prepared for publication, the same process might have been used. The aquatint reproductive technique was a relatively recent invention, having first appeared in France in the 1760s and then been introduced into England by the watercolorist Paul Sandby in 1775. A refinement of the etching process, aquatint allowed for a close duplication of the appearance of wash drawings, which could then be colored by hand. Stylistically the aquatint was especially well suited to the demands of the topographic illustration, which, as noted, was becoming increasingly popular at the same time. In executing drawings intended for translation into aquatints, the artist first established his composition in pencil or ink and then added areas of shading by laying down a thin wash of sepia. Over this monochromatic layer he then proceeded to wash in thin areas of watercolor, concentrating not so much on patches of "local" color as upon broader areas of tonality. The completed drawings would be turned over to professional etchers to be translated into aquatints, with color being applied by hand to match that of the original drawing. The varying stages of "finish" seen in Middleton's drawings for *The Roman Remains* afford an opportunity to follow the artist's steps in fulfilling these procedures.

Middleton was, no doubt, familiar with most of the techniques of printmaking. A number of his landscape sketches in the Middleton Place collection show signs of having been used to transfer the image to plates for engraving. In addition, Eliza Falconnet Middleton wrote from Naples in 1819 that concurrent with John Izard Middleton's stay with her family, she had been learning the process of lithography to record local scenes, "[t]he most tedious part of which is the cuttery of the pencil, which being of a soft composition constantly breaks against the stone" (letter to Mary Hering Middleton, 12 September 1819, Middleton Family Papers). Artists and amateurs alike often prepared single prints or small portfolios as presentation pieces for friends and colleagues. Middleton's delight in traveling to ancient sites, his large circle of friends and relatives, and the evidence of two volumes of drawings would tend to substantiate his varied and active career as a printmaker, but little physical evidence remains.

Middleton executed each of his drawings on-site. Avoiding the older studio process, his work in the field gave to each of his compositions its sense of both accuracy and immediacy. In executing his drawings Middleton relied on the mechanical assistance of a portable camera obscura. He made little compositional alteration to what the lens of this device projected upon his page. Today, when freedom of expression is prized among artists, Middleton's freely admitted dependence on the reproductive contrivance of the camera obscura may seem unusual and even "unartistic." But for him use of this device was a point of pride and a warranty guaranteeing to his readers the truth of what he presented. This drawing apparatus was invented in 1540 and refined by the late seventeenth century into a portable device that was, thereafter, commonly used by both professional and amateur artists, especially in the rendition of plein air landscapes. A boxlike "darkroom" or camera obscura was set up, complete with curtains to enclose the draftsman. Originally a pinhole was poked through one wall of the box, through which the light projected the inverted image beyond onto the opposite wall. Later the addition of sets of mirrors further redirected the image, right-side-up, down onto the horizontal drawing surface so that the artist could trace the outlines of the projected scene. By Middleton's day, a bellows allowed a precise focusing of the image upon the drawing paper, and the apparatus could be transported into the field as a compact package measuring about 18 by 20 inches and only some 4 inches thick. On-site it could be quickly unfolded and set up. Essentially, the camera obscura used the same principle upon which the modern photographic camera depends, lacking only the fixative to "capture" the image permanently. The use of the camera obscura was, as has been noted, appreciated by Norton as evidence of Middleton's scientific commitment, and that scholar was certainly correct in placing Middleton in the forefront of a more modern approach to the science of archaeology. The camera obscura ensured a visual accuracy almost photographic in detail, and in the days before the photograph this was exactly what was desired by the scholarly audience for whom Middleton's views largely were intended. It was not until 1840 and the arrival in Rome of the English daguerreotypist Alexander Ellis that a photographic record of the city's antiquities began to be made. Ellis's initial forays with the photographic lens would soon be followed by the efforts of several celebrated studios, including those of James Anderson (from 1849), the Alinari Brothers (from 1852), and Giocomo Brogi (from 1860). No longer would pencil, pen, and brush be needed for visual reproduction.

Middleton's forty-nine previously unpublished views, chiefly of Rome and its environs—*The Roman Remains,* as they have been titled—take us beyond the purely archaeological theme of the *Grecian Remains* (devoted as it was almost exclusively to pre-Roman antiquity) to present a medley of visual impressions, some ancient, some medieval or Renaissance, and some even contemporary. Ancient ruins do dominate eighteen of the drawings, but the remainder may better be classed as landscape studies. Select views of a Tuscan spa resort and the Savoyard country retreats of two literary giants of the recent past are also included. In some of his depictions Middleton retains the coldly studied vision of the academic; in others his renditions are decidedly more evocative, and even romantic. Accuracy, before the advent of photography, may have been Middleton's primary aim. Yet in examining the several stages of "finish" in the present volume, one must note how Middleton retouched his lines—intensifying some, adding shadows here, deepening the foliage there; this is where evidence of Middleton the artist can be found. As he earlier noted in his introduction to the *Grecian Remains:* "The greater part of my outlines, indeed I may say all the distances, and those parts of the picture which required the accuracy of the antiquary more than the grace of the artist, are done in the same manner [using the camera obscura]. I afterwards retouched them on the spot, and gave that grace of detail which it was impossible to attain while the paper was under the lens."

If the forty-nine scenes presented here were ever intended for publication as a sequel to Middleton's first volume of views, that book, for whatever reason, never materialized. At some point, however, the drawings were mounted on paper backings, for the most part identified by locations (on the reverse), assigned plate numbers, and bound together between red-colored boards embossed on the cover with the name "M. I. I. MIDDLETON." It would seem that Middleton himself had put the drawings into the untitled volume, perhaps to show to a publisher. It is possible, however, that this was done at a later date, since the blue-ink numbering of the drawings is similar to that used to write the name "Mrs. W. M. Neal" (a later owner?) on the front sheet of the volume. Although it was still customary to lay drawings down in an album, the manner in which this particular collection was prepared would suggest a purpose beyond simple preservation, perhaps preparation for publication. In any case, the drawings were kept between their album covers, preserved unnoticed until they were found a few years ago immured within the closet walls of a house in "upcountry" South Carolina, in Greenville, once briefly in the possession of Middleton's older brother, Gov. Henry Middleton. Having come to the attention of Professor and Mrs. David Rembert of Columbia, South Carolina, this volume of Middleton's drawings was donated to the South Caroliniana Library of the University of South Carolina in 1994.

Although the drawings were remarkably well preserved, it was deemed prudent to separate the sheets from the album, detach them from their acidic and potentially destructive backings, and remove whatever blemishes time had caused. This procedure was entrusted to Pamela Randolph, paper conservator for Colonial Williamsburg. Once returned to the South Caroliniana Library, the drawings were framed for exhibition. The original album cover has been preserved and now contains photographic facsimiles of the drawings in the sequence in which they originally appeared at the time of the donation. As published here, the ordering of the drawings differs somewhat from the original arrangement. This change provides a more systematic topographical arrangement. A concordance of old and new plate numbers is included, where relevant, with each entry in this edition.

In the unfortunate absence of Middleton's own text and in order to give a flavor of the descriptive, often ekephrastic, writing of Middleton's day, a selection of relevant quotations has been appended to each entry in the catalogue. It is hoped that through the eyes of Middleton's contemporaries, the modern reader might achieve a better appreciation not only of what Middleton saw but of how he saw it and how he made his visual choices. Most of these excerpts come from the period circa 1800 to 1865, the intention being to include as many as possible from the very years in which Middleton was at work on the drawings. Some of these passages are by well-known literary figures, some were written by travel-book authors, and some are just the comments of persons passing through the area. Together they merge into the record of an early-nineteenth-century encounter with Rome and its environs as faithfully depicted by the pencil and pen of John Izard Middleton.

The drawings published in this volume would seem to have been given their verbal echo by one of Rome's most devoted nineteenth-century American admirers, the author William Wetmore Story, who wrote in his *Roba di Roma* of 1856: "No one lives long in Rome without loving it: and I must, in the beginning, confess myself to be in the same category. . . . These little sketches may remind some of happy days spent under the Roman sky, and, by directing the attention of others to what they have overlooked, may open a door to a new pleasure. *Chi sa?*" It is in that spirit of discovery and memorializing that this first presentation of *The Roman Remains* of John Izard Middleton is now offered.

Catalogue of Middleton's *Roman Remains*

Charles R. Mack

PLATE #1

Ponte Molle on the Tiber
1822
Camera obscura pencil tracing, 9⁷/₈ x 13⁷/₁₆ inches
Initialed and dated lower right

The first of Middleton's album drawings depicts the Ponte Molle with the hillside of the Monte Mario beyond as seen from the southern bank of the Tiber looking west (from the approximate site of the present-day Ponte Flaminio).

The Ponte Molle or, more properly, the Ponte Milvio (Milvian Bridge) was built by the censor M. Aemilius Scaurus in 109 B.C. A short distance to the north, the road it carried out of Rome branched into the Via Cassia and the Via Flaminia. The bridge was rebuilt in the mid fifteenth century under Popes Nicholas V and Calixtus III, the latter adding the watchtower (perhaps incorporating one erected at the end of the third century by the emperor Aurelian). The *ponte* was restored yet again in 1815 under Pius VII, who commissioned from Giuseppe Valadier the triumphal arch at the northern end. During the Italian struggle for unification, it was blown up in 1849 by Garibaldi to slow down the advance of the French army on Rome; it was ordered rebuilt the next year by Pius IX.

The Ponte Molle has witnessed a number of significant historical events. In 63 B.C. Cicero captured the delegates of the Allobroges, who were conspiring with Cataline, here. In A.D. 312 the defeated emperor Maxentius fell from the bridge after Constantine's victory over him at the Saxa Rubra some four miles to the north. It is this battle that ensured the imperial throne for Constantine the Great and the official recognition of the Christian religion. On 13 April 1462 it was the site at which the humanist Pope Pius II received the sacred relic of the head of Saint Andrew from the representatives of the last Byzantine ruler, an event which had great spiritual and political significance.

The Ponte Molle has always been regarded as the unofficial northern gateway to the city of Rome. Most visitors from the north (if not arriving by sea at Civitavecchia) came down either the Via Cassia or the Via Flaminia to cross the Tiber by this bridge, located only two and a half kilometers from the entrance to the city at the Porta del Popolo. During Middleton's day the bridge was the site of an annual festival of the Roman artists' association, at which occasions new members were initiated accompanied by much eating and drinking. Most of the city's foreign contingent of painters and sculptors were members, but Middleton's artistic intentions were perhaps too studious for such frivolities.

1800

It is with a pleasure enlivened by the importance of antiquities to history, and of the history of Rome to that of man, that we undertake to describe every part of this interesting and celebrated city. And in order to arrange so amazing a variety of objects in the most convenient method . . . we shall begin with the Tiber, which the Roman history has rendered so famous, and which the travellers of most nations must pass before they enter Rome. . . . There are five ancient bridges over this river: the first, called the Ponte Molle, nearly two miles on this side of the city, is of simple structure: over this bridge the victorious generals passed on their return to Rome from the conquered kingdoms and provinces, bringing kings and captains prisoners in their train; as also did the tributaries, who came to do homage to the Senate and People. The ancient name of this bridge was Pons Emilianus, from Emilius the censor, who built it; but it was afterwards corrupted into Ponte Milvio, and at length into Ponte Molle. Of the ancient structure no more remains than the tower built by Belisarius, and the piers, on which Nicholas V. rebuilt the bridge: it was destroyed in the battle between Constantine and Maxentius, who was drowned here. The road over it was much frequented by Nero, and rendered famous by the martyrdom of many saints. On the bridge is venerated a small picture of the blessed Virgin, and a statue of St. John Nepomucenus, done by Agostino Cornacchini, by order of Cardinal Alvato.

J. Salmon,
An Historical Description of Ancient and Modern Rome I, pp. 13–14.

1822

Whither he was going he knew not; yet it seemed as if motion gave him the power of enduring what he could not bear at rest; and he continued to traverse street after street, till, quitting the city, he had reached Ponte Molle, where, exhausted by heat and fatigue, he was at length compelled to stop. . . . A desolate vacancy now spread over him, and, leaning over the bridge, he seemed to lose himself in the deepening gloom of the scene, till the black river that moved beneath him appeared almost a part of his mind, and its imageless waters but the visible current of his own dark thoughts.

Washington Allston,
Monaldi, pp. 138–40.

1823

Until we reached the Ponte Molle I saw nothing that indicated the approach to a great city. All was silence and solitude; and the few clumps of shrubs, that occasionally skirted the road, seemed to us as untenanted by birds, as the country around by people. The Tiber, as seen at the Ponte Molle, agreeably surprised me; for instead of being a narrow and turbid stream, as I had been taught to expect, it showed itself as a bold and rapid river, somewhat yellow in its tint it is true, but nevertheless a considerable river, and not a stream.

Countess of Blessington (Marguerite Gardiner),
The Idler in Italy, II, p. 97.

After riding a little more than a mile, we reach the Milvian Bridge, a portion of which is ancient. We will not cross at this spot, so celebrated for the battle fought by Constantine near it, but pursue our way of the side of the stream, on which we still are. Crossing the highway, then, (the ancient Flaminian Way) we continue our course up the river, which just here has been the scene of a melancholy event, of no distant occurrence. The horse of a young Englishwoman backed off the steep bank, and falling over her, she was drowned. What has rendered this calamity more striking, was the fate of her father, who is said to have left a post-house in the mountains, on foot, while traveling, and has never since been found.

James Fenimore Cooper,
Gleanings from Europe, p. 213.

PLATE #2

Fountain of the Acqua Acetosa on the Tiber
1822
Camera obscura pencil tracing, $9^{1}/_{2}$ x $13^{1}/_{2}$ inches
Initialed and dated lower right

The Fonte dell'Acqua Acetosa was a mineral spring located along the south bank of the Tiber about a mile upstream from the Ponte Molle. Its architectural wellhead was long attributed to the baroque sculptor and architect Gian Lorenzo Bernini but now is believed to have been designed by the painter Andrea Sacchi in 1661 on commission from Pope Alexander VII.

Middleton was but one of many artists to sketch this area along the Tiber north of Rome below the slope of Monte Parioli. The site was favored by the Dutch Romanist artists of the seventeenth century as well as by French painters such as Claude Lorrain and Nicholas Poussin. So much did Poussin utilize views of the area in his landscapes that the locale about the Acqua Acetosa was nick-named the "Valle del Pussino" (Poussin's Valley). Today the area, located off the busy Viale di Parioli, is practically overrun by the urban growth of Rome; the fountain is contiguous to one of the city's major athletic facilities.

Among the many who came to sample the vinegary but healing waters at the Acqua Acetosa was the German visitor Goethe, who, in the summer of 1787, would "get up at dawn and walk to the Acqua Acetosa, a mineral spring about half an hour's walk from the Porta del Popolo, where I live. There I drink the water, which tastes like a weak *Schwalbacher,* but is very effective. I am home again by eight, and set to work in whatever way the spirit dictates. My health is excellent" (Goethe, *Italian Journey,* p. 355).

1800

> To the right is an arched way, with an image of the blessed Virgin, under the care of a hermit. Through this, at a little distance, is the celebrated Acqua Acetosa, so called from its acid qualities, and esteemed useful in many disorders.
>
> J. Salmon,
> *An Historical Description of Ancient and Modern Rome* I, p. 16.

PLATE #3

Distant View of the Vatican, Rome
1822
Pencil drawing worked up over camera obscura tracing, 9³/₄ x 7¹/₈ inches
Initialed and dated lower right

Although the precise location of Middleton's vantage point has not been determined, he was perhaps drawing Saint Peter's Basilica as it is seen from the gardens of the Villa Doria Pamphili (Belrespiro) on the Via Aurelia Antica outside the Porta San Pancrazio. More precisely, he may have set up his drawing board along the Via Cava Aurelia, just below the walls of the estate, now one of Rome's most lovely public parks.

1804–5

St. Peter's is a work of man which produces on the mind the effect of a marvel of nature. It is the only work of art on earth which has the kind of grandeur that characterizes the immediate works of creation. In it the genius of man is glorified by the magnificence of nature. . . . The view of such a monument is as a fixed and never-ceasing strain of music—ready to do you good whenever you approach it.

Madame de Staël,
quoted in Abel Stevens, *Madame de Staël*, I, p. 365.

1805

Her swelling domes, her nodding towers rise majestically from the plain and appear like mighty monuments of former greatness.

Washington Irving,
The Complete Works of Washington Irving, I, p. 261.

1853

When Rome is viewed from a distance, the dome of St. Peter's is the central point of observation, and seems to be gathering the rest of the city under its enormous wings. It is so with thoughts and associations. St. Peter's is the first object of interest, around which all others group themselves. Here the traveler hurries as soon as the dust of the journey is shaken from his feet; and here he comes, at the last moment, as the spot from which he is most reluctant to part.

George Stillman Hillard,
Six Months in Italy, I, p. 205.

PLATE #4

Appia Felix Ad Lacum
1822
Pencil drawing worked up over camera obscura tracing, $9^1/_2$ x $13^1/_2$ inches
Initialed and dated lower right

This is the first of eight studies in the Borghese Gardens. Encompassing an area of some seventeen hundred acres, the gardens of the Villa Borghese form Rome's largest park. The villa and its property were the early-seventeenth-century creation of Cardinal Scipione Caffarelli Borghese, the nephew of Pope Paul V, whose manners and elegance earned him the sobriquet of "Rome's Delight." Both the interior of the Cardinal's Casino (which now houses the magnificent art collection of the Galleria Borghese) and the surrounding gardens were vastly transformed in the late eighteenth century.

The formal, baroque gardens of the villa were redesigned in the manner of an English landscaped park in 1773 by Prince Marcantonio Borghese. He commissioned the work from Scottish landscape painter Jacob More, who collaborated with Giulio Camporese (1754–1840) on the project. They were assisted by the architects Antonio and Mario Asprucci and the painter Cristoforo Unterberger, who erected a series of artificial ruins and fountains in a romanticized park setting that stressed the new, more naturalistic English-style approach to landscape architecture. In the 1830s the gardens of the Villa Borghese absorbed those of the adjoining Villa Giustiniani and were somewhat altered under the direction of Luigi Canina. Although open for public enjoyment, the broad vistas, romantic "ruins," fountains, and avenues and paths shaded with oaks, ilexes, and umbrella pines remained in private hands until 1902, when the Borghese Gardens passed into the possession of King Umberto I, who donated the park to the city of Rome.

Middleton's view in this, the first of eight drawings executed within the Borghese Gardens, may have been done looking south across the present-day Piazzale di Canestre into the Viale San Paolo di Brasile toward the Porta Pinciana. The columned entry has disappeared, but the sculpture of the crouching lion remains located at approximately the same site along the Viale Pietro Canonica, which leads to the pseudo-antique temple of Faustina between the Giardino del Lago and the little temple of Diana.

1800

This villa, which once belonged to the Duke Altems, was purchased by Card. Scipio Borghese, nephew of Paul V. who built its most magnificent and highly ornamented casino, after a design of Fiamingo. . . . The house and gardens have been newly fitted up in a most splendid manner by the present prince. The park and the gardens are about three miles in circumference, and are adorned with beautiful fountains and a great number of statues, busts, and termini; temples, lakes, elegant walks, aviaries, grottoes, four hundred pine-trees, groves, shrubberies, etc.

J. Salmon,
An Historical Description of Ancient and Modern Rome, I, pp. 214, 217–18.

1817–18

Villa signifies at Rome a pleasure garden, considerable for extent and magnificence. . . . The villa Borghese, belonging to the prince of that name, situated just without the walls, was formed about 1610, by Cardinal Scipio Borghese, nephew of Paul V. This pope, during a reign of fifteen years, bestowed great riches on his nephews, which their descendents the Borghese family possess at this day. The villa is an extensive piece of ground, three Roman miles in circuit, part of which is laid out with broad walks between hedges of eight to twelve feet high. Another part consists of uneven ground interspersed with trees, having something of the appearance of an English park. There are several roads for driving in carriages through this extensive villa. . . . There are several casinos in the villa, and many ornamental buildings, amongst which are an artificial ruin, representing a temple of Antoninus and Faustina; a temple of Esculapius, surrounded by a piece of water; an imitation of an ancient circus, or hippodrome. There are, in different parts of the ground, statues, ancient inscriptions, old sepulchral monuments, and fountains. The conduit of the Acqua Vergine, one of the three aqueducts that supply Rome, passes through the villa.

W. A. Cadell,
A Journey in Carniola, Italy, and France, I, pp. 232–34.

1828–30

The grounds a little farther beyond, and which show factitious ruins, statues, walks, avenues, and plantations, are the celebrated Villa Borghese, which, by the liberality of the owner are converted into a Hyde Park, or a Bois de Boulogne, for Rome and her visitors. It is said the public has used them so long, that it now claims them as its own; the public in Rome being just as soulless, ungrateful, and rapacious as the public in America. God help the man (if Honest) who depends on the public anywhere.

James Fenimore Cooper,
Gleanings from Europe, pp. 201–2.

I went afterwards to the Villa Borghese, outside the Porto del Popolo. The gardens occupy thirty or forty acres, and are always thronged in the afternoon with the carriages of the Roman and foreign nobility. In summer, it must be a heavenly place; even now, with its musical fountains, long avenues, and grassy slopes crowned with the fan-like branches of the Italian pine, it reminds one of the fairy landscapes of Boccaccio.

Bayard Taylor,
Views A-Foot, pp. 428–29.

PLATE #5

Lake and Temple of Aescalapis in Villa Borghese
1822
Pencil drawing worked up over camera obscura tracing, 9¹/₂ x 13¹/₂ inches
Initialed and dated lower right

The Giardino del Lago features an idyllic artificial pond within the overall landscape of the Borghese Park. An island in the *laghetto* (little lake) supports an imitation Greek temple dedicated to Aescalapius, the ancient god of healing; it was designed in 1786 by Antonio Asprucci with statues in the antique manner by Agostino Penna and Vincenzo Pacetti. Ducks still paddle the waters, and the view has changed little since Middleton's day.

1807

Oswald and Corinne ended their Roman journey at the Villa Borghese where, of all the Roman gardens and palaces, the splendors of nature and the arts are gathered with the most taste and brilliance. Trees of all kinds and magnificent waterways are to be found there. An unbelievable collection of statues, of vases, of stone coffins from ancient times mingle with the freshness of youthful nature in the south. The mythology of the ancients seems to take new life there. Naiads are set on the banks of streams, nymphs in woods worthy of them, tombs in Elysian shade; the statue of Aesculapius stands in the middle of an island; that of Venus seems to be emerging from the shadows. Ovid and Virgil stroll in this lovely place thinking they were still in the Augustan Age. . . . Through the trees you can glimpse the city of Rome in the distance, and Saint Peter's, and the countryside, and long arcades—remains of aqueducts that used to transport mountain streams into ancient Rome. Everything is there for thought, for imagination, for reverie. The purest sensations blend with the pleasures of the soul and so suggest the idea of perfect happiness.

Madame de Staël,
Corinne, pp. 87–88.

PLATE #6

Temple of Aesculepus in the Villa Borghese
1822
Pencil drawing worked up over camera obscura tracing, 9½ x 13½ inches
Initialed and dated lower right

1816–17

> At the left at the end of an avenue, bordered with copies of antique statues, is a beautiful lake, the banks of which are shaded with poplars and osiers. On an island in the midst of this lake rises a beautiful Ionick temple dedicated to Esculapius, whose open and airy portico affords a view of a statue of the god. But alas! the son of Apollo is here stationed in vain, nor can his presence drive away the 'pale Quartana,' a sickly, an emaciated daemon that haunts this delightful abode. The malaria that renders the *Campagna del Roma,* almost uninhabitable, during a greater part of the summer, reigns in all its malignancy at the villa Borghese. I know not whether I was filled with more regret or surprise upon being told, that this superb villa . . . was during the most beautiful months of the year abandoned by its inhabitants. It was with difficulty that I could associate in my imagination, the melancholy thought of disease, with a sun so resplendent and an atmosphere so soft and voluptuous. The gay profusion of flowers that wasted
>> their sweetness on the desert air.'—
>
> —its tall groves of cypress murmuring with the breeze, the incessant warbling of birds and play of fountains, realized, more than any thing I had ever seen, the fairy solitudes of Calypso and Armida.
>
> James Sloan,
> *Rambles in Italy,* pp. 350–51.

1818

> There are indeed cut trees and stagnant pools in the Borghese garden, temples to the God of Health stuck up in the middle of greenish water; but there is also enough of nature to induce us to forgive these wretched attempts at artificial beauty.
>
> Louis Simond,
> *A Tour of Italy and Sicily,* p. 321.

PLATE #7

Modern Ruin in the Villa Borghese [The Temple of Faustina]
1822
Pencil drawing worked up over camera obscura tracing, 9½ x 13½ inches
Initialed and dated lower right

This mock ruin, erected in 1792, was another of the neoclassical adornments to the romanticized landscape architecture of the Villa Borghese Gardens. The "Temple of Faustina" continues to fool the casual visitor today just as it did the American tourist Theodore Dwight in 1821. The archaeological eye of John Izard Middleton, however, was not deceived.

1821

But the most impressive sight of all, and indeed one that had much of majesty in it, was the portico of an ancient temple, deeply wounded by the hand of time and the storms of many a barbarous age, but still retaining a half-obliterated inscription, and wearing in its stature and its frown the air of unquestionable nobility. These tall pillars, and their ponderous frieze, had probably been transported from some distant ruins, but at a little distance they seemed to mark the site of some ancient temple of great magnificence; and while we rambled about these delightful grounds, enjoying the warmth and serenity of the weather, they suddenly made their appearance from time to time, to call the mind to sublime ideas of the period which produced them, and of the ages that have since come and passed away.

Theodore Dwight,
A Journal of a Tour in Italy, pp. 250–51.

1843

In another part of the park is a fac-simile of a small Roman temple dedicated to Faustina, the peristyle consisting of 2 granite columns with their ancient Corinthian capitals, and with copies before it of the Greek inscriptions, now at the Louvre, found on the site of the Villa of Herodes Atticus, on the Via Appia.

John Murray,
Murray's Handbook of Rome and Its Environs, p. 327.

PLATE #8

Within [illegible] *of the Villa Borghese*
1822
Pencil drawing worked up over camera obscura tracing, 9¹⁄₂ x 13¹⁄₂ inches
Initialed and dated lower right

Middleton's view was taken from the Via di Valle Giulia on the slope of the Borghese Gardens; he was looking across the Giulia valley toward a *villino* (cottage) that still exists today along the Viale Giardino Zoologica across from the present-day entrance to the Rome City Zoo. Despite the occasionally heard roar of a distant lion or the chatter of monkeys, the situation seems little changed from what Middleton found.

1821

But we had already arrived at the Borghese Villa, and were approaching the Casino, or little palace, along a winding path frequently overshadowed by evergreens and ornamented with statues both ancient and modern. The grounds are undulating, and about three miles in circuit, beautifully diversified with woods and lawns, where a few deer are seen, and abounding with many monuments of the taste of its previous possessors.

Theodore Dwight,
A Journal of a Tour in Italy, p. 250.

1822

Our usual haunt is the garden of the Villa Borghese. In this delightful spot we find shade and privacy, or sunshine and society, as we may feel inclined. Today it was intensely hot; and we found the cool and sequestered walks and alleys of cypress and ilex, perfectly delicious. I spread my shawl upon a green bank, carpeted with violets, and lounged in most luxurious indolence. . . . The soft air, the trickling and murmuring of innumerable fountains, the urns, the temples, the statues—the localities of the scene— all dispose the mind to a kind of vague but delightful reverie to which we 'find no end, in wandering mazes lost.' In these gardens we frequently meet the Princess Pauline; sometimes alone but oftener surrounded by a cortege of beaux. . . . She is still in deep mourning for the Emperor.

Anna Jameson,
Diary of an Ennuyée, p. 285.

PLATE #9

Fountain in the Villa Borghese
1822
Pencil drawing worked up over camera obscura tracing, 9¹/₂ x 13¹/₂ inches
Initialed and dated lower right

The Fontana dei Cavalli Marini (Fountain of the Sea Horses) has been thought by some to be by Bernini; but, although clearly inspired by the fountains of that baroque master, in actuality it was based on a 1791 design by Cristofero Unterberger. Writing in her *Fountains of Papal Rome* of 1915, Mrs. Charles Mac Veagh noted that this delightful fountain "stands on the summit of a rising avenue, yet does not terminate a vista, it makes itself a part of one, for the avenue continues after the fountain has been reached. It stands in full but tempered sunlight, girt about by a circle of box hedges and ilex trees, with here and there a tall stone pine."

1818

Some of the country villas about Rome, although situated on higher ground than the Seven Hills, are rendered unhealthy by the quantity of water brought thither in pipes, to supply their foolish jets d'eau and cascades, and then suffered to soak into the ground or stagnate: I shall mention only the Borghese, and the Pamfili villas. The former, situated just outside the city gate *del Popolo,* contains about six hundred acres of ground, sufficiently varied with hill and dale, and planted with evergreen oaks, and stone pines, now about two hundred years old. These pines are peculiar to Roman landscape; their umbrella-shaped heads, thick and dark, yet tipped with lively touches of green, and borne on palm-like stems, one hundred feet high, have a formal yet picturesque effect. . . . It is about one hundred years since water was conveyed to these villas, and with it intermittent fevers, which were unknown before.

Louis Simond,
A Tour of Italy and Sicily, pp. 321–22.

1858

We were glad to emerge from the casino into the warm sunshine; and, for my part, I made the best of my way to a large fountain, surrounded by a circular stone seat of wide sweep, and sat down in a sunny segment of the circle. Around grew a solemn company of old trees,—ilexes, I believe,— with huge, contorted trunks and evergreen branches, . . . deep groves, sunny openings, the airy gush of fountains, marble statues, dimly visible in recesses of foliage, great urns and vases, terminal figures, temples,—all these works of art looking as if they had stood there long enough to feel at home, and to be on friendly and familiar terms with the grass and trees. It is a most beautiful place, . . . and the Malaria is its true master and inhabitant!

Nathaniel Hawthorne,
Passages from the French and Italian Note-Books, p. 177.

PLATE #10

Villa Borghese [Temple of Diana]
1822
Pencil drawing worked up over camera obscura tracing, $8^{11}/_{16}$ x $12^{5}/_{8}$ inches
Initialed and dated lower left

Situated on the Viale della Casina di Raffaello within the gardens of the Villa Borghese, this lovely little temple was set up as a visual focus in 1789 as part of the classicizing decoration of the redesigned landscape.

1821

There is a little temple of Diana, and one of Aesculapius, a lake, an aqueduct, and several fountains. Unfrequented paths lead off to different parts of the grounds, and are so tastefully decorated, that almost every turn introduced us to something agreeable and unexpected. Indeed, the succession of busts and vases, fountains spurting from the mouths of animals, gloomy shades whitened with ancient mutilated statues, and open spots affording glimpses of a distant landscape—each came up to view like a new page in some engaging author, leading the mind from one train of thought to another without any exertion of its own.

Theodore Dwight,
A Journal of a Tour in Italy, p. 250.

PLATE #11

Favorite study of the Roman artists in the Villa Borghese
1822
Pencil drawing worked up over camera obscura tracing, 11¼ x 9¼ inches
Initialed and dated lower right

This Borghese garden structure has not been located but may well exist within the private grounds of the Villa Strohl Fern.

1816–17

It was a source of no little surprise to me, to find the villas in the neighborhood of Rome unfrequented, except by a few straggling visitors, who, like myself, were carried to those places by the strong impulse of curiosity. If the Villa *Borghese* were in the neighborhood of Paris or London, it would be crowded from morning till night.

James Sloan,
Rambles in Italy, p. 353.

1847–48

Passing the old gate [the Porta del Popolo] and turning to the right you enter the Villa Borghese, whose gates the munificence of the prince throws open daily to the public. Here you may saunter for hours amid fountains, statues, temples, noble Italian pines, firs, cypresses, ilexes and oaks, and flower beds. Here go the entire fashionable world in gay carriages; yet here are deep green secluded retreats. Here stands the Casino, embowered in roses, and containing works of art. Here you pass Raphael's house and the picturesque Villa Cenci—both long since untenanted and in mournful decay. Near the Borghese is the old deserted Villa Poniatowski. Here in fine weather go English lady tourists to sketch, and landscape painters to make studies of the large aloes and bits of garden ornament which decorate the place.

Christopher Pearse Cranch, as quoted in Leonora Cranch Scott,
The Life and Letters of Christopher Pearse Cranch, p. 123.

Plate #12 [old #15]

Court of the Museum Capitolium
 [The Courtyard of the Palazzo dei Conservatori; south wall view]
1822
Camera obscura pencil tracing, 9½ x 13½ inches
Initialed and dated lower right

Like the Acropolis of Athens, the saddle-shaped Capitoline Hill (the *Campidoglio*) served as the citadel of early Rome; here were its fortified *arx* and its chief temples, that of Jupiter Capitolinus on one height and that of Juno on the other. Today the magnificent trapezoidal piazza of Michelangelo and its adjoining buildings occupy the depression between the two sites. With the demise of imperial grandeur, the once noble hill sank into a medieval squalor, somewhat revived in the twelfth century when a fortified palace was constructed atop the ruins of the ancient Tabularium (the Roman state archives) to house the newly created civil magistracy. This Senators' Palace was joined in the mid fifteenth century by the Conservators' Palace, constructed by Pope Nicholas V to accommodate an additional group of magistrates. Despite these attempts at renewal, the site proved a muddy embarrassment when the Holy Roman emperor Charles V visited the city in 1536. Shortly thereafter Pope Paul III initiated a massive project to restore the Capitoline, commissioning Michelangelo to redesign the Senators' Palace, reconstruct the Conservators' Palace and create a matching building opposite it. Work was continued after the master's death by his executor Giacomo della Porta, followed by Martino Longhi and Girolamo Rinaldi. It was not until 1654 that work was completed. Almost from the first, the Conservators' Palace and its twin were used to house various works of antique art as a sort of civic counterpart to the papal collections in the Vatican. Today the two buildings are entirely given over to the functions of museums.

Looking monolithically Mussolini-like in their impassive grandeur, the two great heads depicted in this drawing, now known to represent Constantine the Great and Constantius II, were thought in Middleton's day to be portraits of the earlier emperors Domitian and Commodus. It is interesting to note how little attention they were accorded by nineteenth-century commentators. They are certainly more appreciated by the modern visitor who views them with eyes opened by this century's experiences with totalitarianism. For Middleton's contemporaries their dehumanizing bearing would have clashed with preconceived ideas of the classical past. The eight-foot-high marble head of Constantine, at the left foreground of Middleton's view, together with portions of his arm, leg, hand, and feet were transported here in the fifteenth century from the Basilica Nova, where they had once formed part of a gigantic seated statue of the emperor more than thirty feet high. At the far left, and of almost equal size, is the great bronze head of the youthful Constantius II. In the niche to the rear is a seated statue of the goddess Roma dating from the time of Trajan in the early

second century, together with statues of barbarian prisoners and Egyptian deities. Despite the enormity of the sculptures and their substantial weight (the head of Constantine being estimated at eight tons), there has been considerable relocating of the works since Middleton's day. The fragments of Constantine's statue are now positioned directly across from their 1820s location.

1800

In the palace on the right the Roman magistrates assemble and give audience. The rooms under the portico are appropriated to an accademy of arts. . . . At the further end of the court-yard, under the portico, which is by Buonarotti, is the statue of Rome sitting, on the pedestal of which, in basso-relievo, are represented the subjugated Dacians. To the right and left are two captive kings without hands, of admirable workmanship, in black marble: also two Egyptian idols, found at the Porta Salaria. In the court-yard are two colossal heads, one in Grecian marble of Domitian, the other in metal of Commodus, and a hand of the same.

J. Salmon,
An Historical Description of Ancient and Modern Rome, I, p. 81.

1801–02

Within a gloomy Court, you again see a Roma Triumphans, attended by conquered Provinces—a Lion devouring a Horse—and two prodigious Heads, two feet, and one hand, of colossal Statues of Commodus and Domitian, mutilated by the People on the death of those inhuman Monsters.

Joseph Sansom,
Letters from Europe, p. 389.

1801–03

A Rome Triumphant is seated here on an ancient pedestal well enough proportioned to the figure. . . . The two captive kings are called in the modern inscriptions Numidians, perhaps because the marble is black: some have even baptized them Jugurtha and Syphax. A statue surely does better with a name than without one; but these are breeched in the Parthian anaxyrides, their chlamys seems too full and their faces too fine for Africans.

Joseph Forsyth,
Remarks on Antiquities, Arts, and Letters, pp. 215–16.

1818–19

The continuation of the Museum is in the building opposite, called the Palazzo de'Conservatori. In the court are several fragments of colossal statues; among them a head of Commodus, in bronze, which is said to be the same which that emperor placed upon a colossal statue of Nero. . . . There is also a head of Domitian in marble. A colossal foot belonged to a statue in the Temple of Peace.

Edward Burton,
A Description of the Antiquities and Other Curiosities of Rome, I, pp. 147–48.

Rather glad, perhaps, to have a good reason for mounting to the Capitol again, we divided the business, and visited the Palazzo de'Conservatori another day. There is a tremendously fine group in the quadrangle of a lion that has subdued and is in the act of devouring a horse. I wonder where the artist got his models for this group! . . . He could scarcely have imagined the agony of the one beast and the contented ferocity of the other.

Mrs. Trollope,
A Visit to Italy, II, pp. 324–25.

PLATE #13 [OLD #16]

Court of the Museum Capitolium
[The Courtyard of the Palazzo dei Conservatori; north wall view]
1822
Camera obscura pencil tracing, 9½ x 13½ inches
Initialed and dated lower right

At the end of the courtyard wall, a visitor gazes up at a sculpture famous in the past but ignored in the guidebooks of today: the marble fragment of a lion seizing a horse. It has been mentioned in documents since the second quarter of the fourteenth century and was, perhaps, known a century earlier. Restored in 1594 by the Milanese sculptor Ruggero Bescape, the composition exerted an influence on a variety of later artists, from Jacopo Bellini to Rubens to Delacroix. Today it is to be found in the gardens of the palace.

The notice on the column to the right in Middleton's drawing informs visitors that they need to ring the custodian for admittance to the museum galleries above. Mariana Starke's guidebook of 1833, *Travels in Europe for the Use of Travellers on the Continent,* advised travelers that "admittance may usually be obtained on days when the Museum is not open to the Public, by an application to the Custode; who, if thus called upon, expects a fee" (p. 148).

Modern-day visitors to Rome are advised to take advantage of Saturday evening hours at the museums of the Campidoglio when the illuminations show off the collections of antiquities contained in the galleries of both the Capitoline and Conservators' Palaces to their romantic best. It is interesting to note that such visits have a long-standing tradition. Starke noted as early as 1801–2 that "Those persons who wish to see the Museums of the Capitol . . . to advantage should visit them by torch-light; as the torch like Promethean fire, makes every statue live. . . . For seeing the museum of the Capitol, two large wax torches are sufficient. . . . It is expected, that every party shall come furnished with wax torches: and it is likewise expected that each party shall give, at the Capitol, to the Custode who shows the statues, and his attendants, from six to eight scudi, provided there be fires in one or two of the apartments . . ." (*Travels in Europe,* p. 148, n.2).

1800

The two feet and a hand, of Greek marble, are supposed to be parts of a colossal statue of Apollo, thirty cubits high. The lion seizing a horse was found in the water near a mill out of the gate of St. Paolo, and is of fine Grecian workmanship. Farther on is a piece of marble on which are delineated the measures of merchants and architects. The sepulchral marble, with the inscription of Agrippina, wife of Germanicus, is said to have contained her ashes.

J. Salmon,
An Historical Description of Ancient and Modern Rome, I, pp. 81–82.

PLATE #14 [OLD #13]

Forum Romanum
1822
Pencil drawing worked up over camera obscura tracing, 9½ x 13½ inches
Initialed and dated lower right

The Roman Forum was the religious, civic, and business center of the ancient city and thus might be considered to have been the hub of the Roman world. Here one came to meet friends, hear the orations of noble senators, listen to judicial cases, offer propitiatory sacrifices at hallowed shrines, purchase foodstuffs, learn the news of far-off legionary expeditions, gossip the latest rumor, and discover the fate of grain shipments from Sicily or distant Egypt. The Forum was the ancient heart of Rome, the vibrant center of the city and her empire.

Originally a swampy valley between the Capitoline, Palatine, Quirinal, and Esquiline Hills, the area was drained in the days of the kings and quickly became the gathering place for the various hilltop settlements that composed the ancient community. By the end of the republic its spaces had been filled in with the glorious brick and marble buildings that as a group acted as the focus of the city. During the empire the once-ample space of the Forum became encumbered with all sorts of commemorative monuments and triumphal arches, so much so that new construction was brought to a virtual halt by the third century. Gradually, over the centuries, the Forum began to yield pride of place to the several imperial forums constructed adjacent to it and the district of the Campus Martius with its centerpiece Pantheon. The collapse of Rome before successive waves of barbarian invaders brought closure to the greatness of the Forum. The sack of her buildings by the Gothic forces of Alaric in 410 was but the first of the depredations. The last temple had been closed in 391 and some of the old pagan shrines converted to Christian use, but most of the pillaged buildings were allowed to fall into disrepair and eventual ruin. Marble facings and sculptures were hacked into building stone or burned for lime as weeds and foliage took over. Columns, arches, and ancient walls either collapsed or sank beneath a growing level of decaying stone and soil, in some places more than sixty feet deep. Feuding medieval families constructed fortifications about several of the ancient monuments, but by the end of the Middle Ages the once-mighty Forum was pasturage for grazing sheep and cows; even in the nineteenth century the nickname of "Campo Vaccino" (the cow field) still had validity.

Excavation of the Forum began sporadically in the eighteenth century (often by curious foreigners who had purchased franchises for such purposes). The first real exploration was begun under the French, and in 1803 serious excavations were initiated under the direction of Carlo Fea followed by several successive

campaigns involving some of the most important names in Roman archaeology. Systematic digs were carried out between 1848 and 1853 and again from 1874 to 1884. A massive archaeological project was undertaken between 1898 and 1922, resulting in the exposure of most of the major monuments.

Today the Foro Romano is an archaeological park, a veritable memory garden populated by excavated ruins through which wander the historical shades of emperors, statesmen, priests and priestesses, merchants, and even Shakespearean orators. They all have taken on a more fleshly existence since the archaeologists began in earnest their work of revelation. When Middleton drew his three views of the Forum he was not able to reconstruct the monumental totality of the area nor to provide a sense of the original architectural composition of the place. The excavations had only begun, and their trenches, pits, and piles of earth only obscured the view. They still continue; the old road that twisted up the back of the Capitoline Hill has been erased by archaeological intervention, and the contiguous Forum of the emperor Nerva is in the course of discovery.

The Forum in Middleton's day was still pretty much the old Campo Vaccino, whose scattered columns and partially revealed arches offered shade to grazing cattle and a hint of nostalgic glory to the visitor. American painters, by and large, tended to avoid the sight, daunted by the painted visions of Claude Lorrain and Pannini as well as by the sweep of pasture, by the disjuncture of the ignoble remains, and, perhaps, by what the ruined state of the place might predict of America's own "manifest destiny" (see Vance, *America's Rome*, I, p. 5). Middleton's scholarly eye, however, did not romanticize or fantasize, and so he was able to record with a literal precision what he saw projected upon his paper.

For this panorama Middleton looked north from what we now know to have been the House of the Vestal Virgins, toward the Capitoline Hill. In the foreground, with a little figure at their base to provide some sense of the enormous scale, stand the three magnificent Corinthian columns of the Temple of the Dioscuri capped by the surviving remnants of their entablature. This is one of the most familiar of the Forum's many monuments. The columns had been pulled down in 1811 but had been re-erected braced with the iron bars that Middleton was careful to render in his view. The Temple of the Dioscuri, with the column bases and towering podium still buried in the 1820s, commemorates the divine twins, Castor and Pollux, who appeared upon the battlefield of Lake Regillus in 496 B.C. to aid the Roman forces against her Latin tribal foes. Through the columns Middleton depicts the rise of the Capitoline Hill and the rear of the Senate House with its high bell tower, erected in 1582 by Martino Longhi. The Senators' Palace rests upon the massive foundations of the ancient Tabilarium, which housed the state records of Rome and whose row of massive arches has been revealed today. To its right can be seen the still half-buried Arch of Septimius Severus (A.D. 203) and, further to the right, the line of trees marking the avenue of Pope Paul III, laid out in 1536 along the path of the ancient Via Sacra to facilitate the passage of the visiting emperor Charles V through the Forum.

Beyond the trees rises the handsome cupola of the Church of Saints Luke and Martin restored by Pietro da Cortona in 1634. Also poking above the trees is the little belfry of the Church of Saint Hadrian built out of the well-preserved fabric of Diocletian's late-third-century Senate House, the Curia, restored in 1937 to its ancient condition. Scattered here and there about Middleton's scene are the mounds of excavated earth, over which several of his contemporaries lamented, and the carts of the diggers.

1807

Readings in history, the thoughts they provoke, do not act upon our souls like these scattered stones, these ruins interspersed with buildings. Eyes are all-powerful over the soul: once you have seen Roman ruins, you believe in the ancient Romans as if you had lived among them. . . . The Forum, so tightly enclosed, witness to so many astonishing things, is striking proof of man's moral grandeur.

Madame de Staël,
Corinne, pp. 64–65.

1817

The Forum was the Cow-field in the beginning of the fifteenth century, and the sacred precincts are usually known by no other name to this day. The accretion of soil is so great in the *Campo Vaccino,* that the excavations to the ancient level have thrown up heaps of earth, the disposal of which has become a matter of difficulty. The dissection has not yet led to a correct anatomy of the ancient structure.

Lord Broughton (John Cam Hobhouse),
Italy, II, p. 60.

1817

Before us is a scene of ruined splendour: massive and grand, and sufficient to strike the spectator with awe even in their present mutilated state. Those monuments which remain are half-buried in their ruins; and the Forum of Rome, where the intellect of the world was concentrated, the seat of universal empire, is converted into a cattle market, with the contemptible designation of Campo Veccino [*sic*]; and the walks of philosophers covered with asses, monks, and straw. Such is the mutability of human affairs.

Henry Sass,
A Journey to Rome and Naples, p. 102.

1817–18

To stand on the grass-grown and deserted spot where Scipio had trod, where Cicero had spoken, where Caesar had triumphed, and where Brutus had acted 'a Roman part,' was all my hope. What then was my astonishment . . . to behold Corinthian columns, ruined temples, triumphal arches, and mouldering walls, not the less affecting from their decay; . . . I stood in the Roman Forum! —Amidst its silence and desertion, how forcibly did the memory of ages that were fled speak to the soul! . . . . Such to me is the charm of being where they have been, that this moment, in which I felt that I stood upon the sacred soil of the Roman Forum, was of itself a sufficient compensation for all the toils and privations, and difficulties and dangers, we had encountered in our long and tedious pilgrimage.

Charlotte Eaton,
Rome in the Nineteenth Century, pp. 123–24.

[The identity of the three Corinthian columns with entablature, now accepted as once forming part of the porch of the Temple of Castor and Pollux, was hotly debated while Middleton was in Rome.]

1817–18

The three beautiful columns near the base of the Palatine Hill . . . have had so many names, that at present, in order to prevent disputes, they are generally called, 'the Disputed Columns'; for, by whatever name you happened to christen them in conversation, it was more than probable that the person you addressed knew them by some other; and, after mutual Explanation, each party secretly pitied or despised the ignorance of his acquaintance. As for instance, somebody mentions the remains of the Temple of Jupitor Stator.

'Jupitor Stator!' exclaims his friend—'Where is it?—I never saw it.'

'Impossible! Never saw the three beautiful columns in the Forum, where they are excavating the marble staircase!'

'O, that is the Temple of Castor and Pollux.'

'I beg your pardon,' interposes a third; 'it is thought, upon the best authority, to be a part of Caligula's bridge.'

'Caligula's bridge!—Nay, that is impossible, however; for it was destroyed nearly as soon as himself. I believe it is now considered a part of the Curia.'

'Say rather the Comitium, which was in front of the Curia,' rejoins another. And so they go on.

Charlotte Eaton,
Rome in the Nineteenth Century, I, pp. 288–89.

1841

Much still remains to be excavated from the ruins of Rome, and, at present, the work goes on slowly. While Rome was an imperial city of the French empire, most was done that has ever been done, and, unless times alter, that ever will be done, by way of exhuming these buried relics of ancient art. There were quite a number of state prisoners, with their wheelbarrows and spades in the Forum; most of them, however, basking or sleeping in the sun.

Wilbur Fisk,
Travels in Europe, p. 293.

The rest of the day we spent digging about in the excavations just below the Capitol. You know that the Temples undergo vaccination [renaming] every 7 years; at the last the eight columns—I am speaking now of directly below the Capitoline wall—were vaccinated with the name of Temple of Fortune; the 3 preserve that of Jupiter Tonans; and the marble floor and remains (of wall and step) close to Jupiter Tonans just behind Septimus Severus, are the Temple of Concord; while the three columns on the other side the Column of Phoca, belonged to the Graeco stadium or Comita, I mean the three so long called Jupiter Stator, but Jupitor Stator, it is now proved, was certainly on the Palatine. . . . You see I am quite coherent at times. But I must go—ever, dearest Mum, Your loving child in haste.

Florence Nightingale,
Florence Nightingale in Rome, pp. 81–82.

Plate #15 [old #14]

Forum Romanum
1822
Pencil drawing worked up over camera obscura tracing with additions of ink
  in foreground, 9½ x 13½ inches
Initialed and dated lower right

In this view Middleton presents the expanse of the Roman Forum from the opposite direction, looking southward from the foot of the Capitoline Hill while standing on the approximate site of the ancient Temple of Concord. In the distance can be seen the three columns marking the Temple of Dioscuri and the artist's vantage point in the previous drawing. Beyond those ancient columns, an assemblage of later buildings, and the Church of Santa Maria Liberatrice (demolished in 1901–2) rises the tree-covered Palatine Hill and the site of the Palace of Tiberius, occupied since the sixteenth century by the lovely Farnese Gardens.

In the immediate foreground stands another set of three fluted Corinthian columns, the sole survivors of a temple dedicated to the emperor Vespasian and his son Titus and dating from the late first century A.D. When Middleton saw them they had been recently (1811) excavated out of the accumulated earth by the architect Giuseppe Valadier. Partly obscured by these columns are the eight thirty-six-foot-high granite Ionic columns marking the porch of the much-rebuilt Temple of Saturn. The first temple to the deity was erected in 497 B.C., and it was here that the annual December Saturnalia took place, a time in which social roles were reversed, slaves had license to mock their owners, and masters were compelled to wait upon their servants. So popular was this festival among the common folk that the Church was forced to keep the holiday, altered into Christmas, in its calendar.

On the left side of the drawing, below the slope of the hill, can be seen the top of the Arch of Septimius Severus. In the middle distance stands the single Column of Phocas, the last monument to be erected in the Forum Romanum. Salvaged from an earlier imperial building, the forty-six-foot-tall column was set up in A.D. 608 by order of the Italian exarch Zmargdus and Pope Boniface IV to honor the Byzantine emperor Phocas. Further to the left is the avenue of trees marking the Via Sacra, which leads to the Arch of Titus and, eventually, past the Church of Saint Francesca Romana to the Coliseum.

1801–2

> The Roman Forum now lay extended before us, a scene in the ages of Roman greatness of unparalled splendor and magnificence. It was bordered on both sides with temples, and lined with statues. It terminated in triumphal arches, and was bounded here by the Palatine hill, with the imperial residence glittering on its summit, and there by the Capitol, with its

ascending ranges of porticos and of temples. Thus it presented one of the richest exhibitions that eyes could behold, or human ingenuity invent. In the midst of these superb monuments, the memorials of their greatness, and the trophies of their fathers, the Roman people assembled to exercise their sovereign power, and to decide the fates of heroes, of kings, and of nations. . . .

But the glories of the Forum are now fled for ever; its temples are fallen; its sanctuaries have crumbled into dust; its colonnades encumber its pavements now buried under their remains. The walls of the Rostra stripped of their ornaments and doomed to eternal silence, a few shattered porticos, and here and there an insulated column standing in the midst of broken shafts, vast fragments of marble capitals and cornices heaped together in masses, remind the traveller, that the field which he now traverses, was once the Roman Forum.

Rev. John Chetwode Eustace,
A Classical Tour through Italy, pp. 435–36.

1807

No doubt all these modern buildings mingled with the ancient debris are intrusive; but a portico standing beside a humble roof, small church windows cut out between columns, . . . evoke an inexplicable mixture of great and simple ideas, an inexplicable pleasure of discovery which keeps us constantly interested. On the outside . . . Rome offers the mournful sight of poverty and degradation. But suddenly a broken column, a half-wrecked bas-relief, stones linked to the indestructible style of ancient architects, remind you that there is an eternal power in man, a divine spark, and that you must never grow weary of lighting it in yourself and of rekindling it in others.

Madame de Staël,
Corinne, pp. 64–65.

1817–18

I seated myself on the fragment of a broken column at the base of the Temple of Concord, and as I gazed on the ruins around me, the remembrance of the scenes their early pride had witnessed, the long lapse of ages, and the fall of tyrants that have since intervened, the contrast of past greatness with present degradation, of ancient virtue and freedom, with existing moral debasement and slavery, forced on my mind, with deeper conviction, the eternal truth, confirmed by the voice of ages, that man is great and prosperous only while he is free; that true glory does not consist in the mere possession of unbounded power or extended empire, but in the diffusion of knowledge, justice, and civilization; . . . But I must restrain my pen, and tell you not what I felt, but what I saw.

Charlotte Eaton,
Rome in the Nineteenth Century, I, pp. 126–27.

1822

The apartment being in an upper story, . . . commanded an extensive view of the southern portion of the city, overlooking the Campo Vaccino, once the ancient forum, with its surrounding ruins, and taking in a part of the Coliseum. The air was hot and close, and there was a thin yellow haze over the distance like that which precedes the scirocco, but the nearer objects were clear and distinct, and so bright that the eye could hardly rest on them without quivering, especially on the modern buildings, with their huge sweep of whited walls, and their red-tiled roofs, that lay burning in the sun, while the sharp, black shadows, which here and there seemed to indent the dazzling masses, might almost have been fancied the cinder-tracks of his fire.

> Washington Allston,
> *Monaldi,* pp. 63–64.

1827

Further on in the Forum stands an isolated column. It is of marble, of Corinthian order, and fluted. Until 1813, this column was regarded as belonging to the temple of Jupiter Custos. On March 13, 1813, one of the last excavations ordered by Napoleon led the workers to the inscription placed eight or ten feet underground, and it was seen that this column had been erected in honor of Phocas, by Smaragdus, exarch of Italy, in the year 608. It bore a statue of the tyrant in gilded bronze.

> Stendhal,
> *A Roman Journal,* p. 95.

1838

And where is the Forum? I see before me a large open space, cleared up by French curiosity. Yonder are halves of some twenty enormous granite columns, still standing and strewed around. I behold fragments of capitals and friezes—the arm of one statue, and the leg of another. These, however, are but the relics of a little part. Still vaster remains are fifteen feet under the earth's surface, beneath those churches and that palace. The curiosity of some coming age may perhaps dig them up.

Truly, a most thorough desolation did those northern Barbarians make, in their destroying enterprises! Not one of those immense columns remains whole. With what fiendish and eager zeal, must they not have gone on, heaping destruction on destruction! For a moment you may seem to see as in some dream, the beautiful porticos, the sacred temple, the triumphal arch, on whose top is a car drawn by four marble steeds, standing out with chiseled distinctness, in the clear sky. The vision changes, and lo, savage forms with fire and sword, are desecrating the heathen fame, and you hear their exulting shouts, as the statue of the Emperor tumbles, from that far height, headlong to the ground. That vision swiftly fades. Temple and tower have gone down. The cries of vanquisher and of vanquished have ceased. A thousand years pass away, and before you is nothing but this melancholy rubbish.

> Isaac Appleton Jewett,
> *Passages in Foreign Travel,* II, pp. 254–55.

PLATE #16 [OLD #12]

Temple of Antoninus and Faustina in the Forum
1822
Pencil drawing worked up in part over camera obscura tracing,
   9³/₈ x 13¹/₂ inches
Initialed and dated lower right

Middleton's view is sighted along the tree-lined Via Sacra (now defoliated by excavation) with the impressive front of the Temple of Antoninus and Faustina shown on the left. Despite her reportedly scandalous behavior, Antoninus Pius revered his wife, and at her death in A.D. 141 this well-respected emperor erected this temple in her memory. At his death, in 161, the temple was rededicated to honor the name of Antoninus as well. At some time, probably late in the tenth century, the Church of San Lorenzo in Miranda took shape within the fabric of the old temple. As part of Pope Paul III's preparation for Charles V's visit of 1536, the facade of this church was set back to reveal the six splendid monolithic Corinthian columns of the temple's portico. In 1602 the church was extensively rebuilt in the style of the early baroque and is still in use today.

By the time the Temple of Antoninus and Faustina was converted into a church, the level of the old Forum had already risen some forty feet to the top of the temple podium, completely covering the flight of twenty-one frontal steps. These were not revealed until the excavations of 1811. In Middleton's drawing this excavation zone can be seen in the fenced-off area just beyond the cart.

Beyond the portico of the Temple of Antoninus and Faustina, Middleton depicts the circular brick structure of the Temple of Romulus, dedicated to the memory of his infant son by the emperor Maxentius in 309. It was Maxentius whom Constantine defeated at the Milvian Bridge three years later. With the advent of Christianity, Pope Felix IV converted the little building, circa 530, into a vestibule for the neighboring Church of Saints Cosmas and Damian. Notable at this late imperial temple are the original bronze doors through which one still enters the building.

Unseen in Middleton's view, beyond the Temple of Romulus lies the impressive structure of the Basilica Nova, started by Maxentius and completed by Constantine, and still erroneously taken in the 1820s for Vespasian's Forum of Peace. Closing off the scene is the facade of the Church of Santa Francesca Romana, built out of the remains of Hadrian's great Temple of Rome and Venus, the last pagan temple to operate in Rome, not having been suppressed until A.D. 391.

A little farther on commences a double range of trees that leads along the Via Sacra by the temples of Antoninus, and of Peace to the arch of Titus. A herdsman seated on a pedestal while his oxen were drinking at the fountain, and a few passengers moving at a distance in different directions, were the only living beings that disturbed the silence and solitude which reigned around. Thus the place seemed restored to its original wildness described by Virgil, and abandoned once more to flocks and herds of cattle. So far have the modern Romans forgotten the theatre of the glory and of the imperial dower of their ancestor, as to degrade it into a common market for cattle, and sink its name illustrated by every page of Roman history into the contemptible appellation of *Campo Vaccino*.

Rev. John Chetwode Eustace,
A Classical Tour through Italy, I, pp. 236–37.

1817–18

The Forum Romanum is now a large open place with a double row of small trees, unpaved, and used as a cattle market; and, therefore, called the Campo Vaccino. It contains many remains of ancient buildings. . . . Farther on . . . is the portico of the Temple of Antoninus and Faustina, erected in 168, by M. Aurelius. This portico consists of ten large columns, each of one piece of Cipollino marble, with Corinthian capitals, and supporting an entablature of large blocks of marble; six of the columns are in front. . . . Behind the portico is the church belonging to the corporation of druggists, Santa Maria in Miranda de'Speziali.

W. A. Cadell,
A Journey in Carniola, Italy, and France, pp. 368–88.

1827

The magnificent temple of Antoninus and Faustina . . . has the advantage of giving the traveler a perfectly clear idea of an ancient temple. This one was on the Via Sacra and, it is said, outside the Forum; the Via Sacra began by the Colosseum and, passing beneath the arch of Titus, before the temple of Antoninus and Faustina, and beneath the arch of Septimius Severus, reached the Capitol by the Clivus Capitolinus. It was on this road, laid out in the midst of the tall trees of a forest, that Romulus and Tatius, king of the Sabines, concluded peace. The sacrifices that were made on this occasion and the religious ceremonies that took place on the Via Sacra gave it its name.

The temple that we are viewing was erected by order of the senate, in honor of Faustina, the young wife of Marcus Antoninus. After this emperor's death, his name was added to the inscription. The porch is formed by ten great columns, each hewn out of a single block of Cipilin marble; they are fourteen feet in circumference and forty-three feet in height. The entablature is composed of immense blocks of marble. This temple, erected in honor of the wife of the reigning sovereign, may serve to give us an idea of Roman magnificence.

Stendhal,
A Roman Journal, pp. 95–96.

At this spot a number of labourers, lazily occupied in the schemes of excavation, have cleared a considerable distance down, exposing to view, at the depth of fifteen feet, the pavement of the ancient *Via Sacra,* which leads towards the Colosseum and the arch of Constantine. . . . The earth which is thus removed, in very small wheel-barrows, from one place is only piled up in another, to be again removed to a third place; for Rome has been so completely filled up by the ruins of the ancient city, and has so little now that requires filling in, that the ingenuity of her engineers cannot find use for this superfluous earth—otherwise, with the labour which is now wasted, the whole forum, from the Capitol to the Colosseum, might be entirely cleared out. The workmen employed here were recently beggars, thus forced into unwanted occupation by the government; or convicts, with chains round their ankles, guarded by lazy soldiers sitting and lounging all day in the sun, or playing cards on a stone.

Rembrandt Peale,
Notes on Italy, pp. 103–4.

PLATE #17 [OLD UNNUMBERED]

No inscription [Interior of the Coliseum by night]
1821
Watercolor with gouache over pencil, 13 x 9½ inches
Initialed, inscribed "Rome," and dated lower right

This painting on paper was loosely laid into Middleton's volume and actually may be superfluous to the album and the projected book. In fact the number "48" written in ink on the end cover of the volume may indicate the maximum number of proposed illustrations. On the other hand, Middleton also may have intended the finish and color of his Coliseum view to serve as a guide for the prospective publisher of his new volume of views.

Theodore Stebbins claims Thomas Cole as "the first of many American landscape painters to choose the Colosseum itself as a subject," but Cole's canvas of circa 1832 postdates Middleton's evocative watercolor by a decade. In this view of the interior of the Coliseum as seen through an arched vault at the southern side of the amphitheater, the black cross dedicated to the memory of Christian martyrs and one of the stations of the cross tabernacles erected by Pope Benedict XIV in 1744 can be glimpsed. These pious memorials were removed in the course of archaeological excavations in the 1870s, which revealed the totality of the substructures beneath the arena floor.

The Flavian amphitheater occupies a low-lying and originally marshy area between the Palatine, Esquiline, and Caelian Hills. As part of his grandiose Golden House estate, the emperor Nero installed an artificial lake at the site and nearby erected a colossal 120-foot-high golden statue of himself as the god Apollo. It was from this statue, called the "Colossus," that the amphitheater eventually took its nickname. The first member of the imperial Flavian dynasty, Vespasian, began the construction of the amphitheater on the site of Nero's lake in A.D. 72 to house the bloody gladiatorial combats that were growing increasingly popular with the Roman citizenry. The building project was completed under Vespasian's sons Titus and Domitian, reaching its final four-story height of 165 feet in A.D. 86. In the inaugural games of A.D. 80, a delighted audience reportedly witnessed the deaths of eleven thousand animals and ten thousand gladiators.

The exterior of the great amphitheater (the ancestor of modern-day baseball and football stadiums in America and the bullrings of Spain) was articulated by superimposed half columns and pilasters in the three ancient orders. The elliptical footprint of the Coliseum measures 616 by 511 feet with an arena floor of 287 by 180 feet. Seating capacity is estimated to have been in excess of fifty thousand. Typically Roman were the smoothly controlled spectator access through eighty arched entrances, convenient staircase ascent to the upper seating levels, and the entire construction based upon the use of concentric and intersecting vaulted corridors that distributed the weight of the massive marble, travertine, brick, and concrete structure.

Christian Rome abolished gladiatorial combats in 404, and the last recorded profane spectacle in the Coliseum was a wild animal hunt staged by one of the Ostragothic princes in 523. In the early Middle Ages the Venerable Bede of England (673–735) reported a saying common among pilgrims to Rome that "While the Coliseum stands, Rome shall stand; when the Coliseum falls, Rome shall fall; and when Rome falls, the world shall fall." The Coliseum lay in disuse, subject to decay and earthquake collapse, until it was temporarily converted into a fortress in 1144 by the Frangipani family. Over the years collapsed and quarried materials from the Coliseum have been used to build and repair much of Rome, including the Vatican and Saint Peter's Basilica. By the time Middleton did this watercolor, Pope Pius VII had already buttressed the outer perimeter of the Coliseum and had begun a process of rehabilitation, thereby reversing centuries of despoliation. During the Napoleonic occupation of Rome, French archaeologists actually had begun excavations in the arena. Despite these recent efforts, Middleton would still have experienced the romance of the stadium and seen the arena floor and the rising tiers of seats covered with verdant foliage creating almost a man-built mountainscape in the middle of Rome. Some of the many species of flora were of exotic origin, perhaps introduced in antiquity in the fodder of the animals brought as victims to the amphitheater. In fact, in 1813 an Italian botanist named Antonio Sebastiani published a *Flora Colisea* enumerating 261 species of plants found among the ruins, a number surpassed by the more than 420 varieties listed in Richard Deakin's *Flora of the Colosseum* of 1855. The archaeological exploration of the Coliseum halted following the French withdrawal but was resumed with an extensive campaign beginning in 1874. William Wetmore Story, who had lauded the overgrown decay of the structure in the earlier editions of his *Roba di Roma*, was forced, in the thirteenth edition of 1887, to note sadly, "The arena, once so peaceful and smoothed over with low grass, has been excavated to exhibit the foundations. . . . All the charm of the place has been destroyed," adding that now the visitor might, "if it pleases you, gaze down into ugly pits and trenches." This enormous task of removal and excavation was not completed until 1940. Today the structural bones of the edifice have been revealed with perfect clarity, but the botanical beauty and sense of mystery have vanished.

While the architectural accomplishments of the Roman builders could best be appreciated in daylight clarity, the nineteenth-century love of romance dictated nocturnal visits in which moonlight could transform the massive skeleton into a structure of infinite mystery. Actually, such evocative visits were long-standing, one of the most famous having been made by the sixteenth-century sculptor Benvenuto Cellini in the company of a necromancing priest with the deliberate intention of conjuring up demonic ghosts (his autobiography claimed success). Witchcraft aside, moonlit visits to the Coliseum are still on tourists' Roman agendas.

Had she lived long enough, one might have imagined Madame de Staël looking over Middleton's shoulder as, almost two decades after her first visit, he painted this romantic view, and reminding him:

> To have seen it only by day is not to know its effect: the brilliant Italian sun lends everything a holiday air, but the moon is the star for ruins. The Amphitheater seems to rise into the skies so that at times, seen through its apertures, some part of heaven's vault looks like a dark blue curtain placed behind the structure. The plants clinging to decaying walls, growing in solitary places, take on the colors of the night; finding itself alone with nature, the soul shudders and has tender feelings all at once. (*Corinne,* p. 286)

William Vance has noted that "we concreate a cumulative American image of the Colosseum that in its complexity expresses an ambivalent attitude toward imperial power, its rise, its glories and terrors, and its fall. The Colosseum becomes the Moby-Dick of architecture, a sublimely multivalent symbol, sacred yet malignant, alien and dreadful yet magnificent, ravaged yet enduring" (*America's Rome,* I, p. 45).

Circa 1800

On a beautiful evening in July last I seated myself at Collisee, on a step of the altar dedicated to the sufferings of the Passion. The sun was setting, and poured floods of gold through all the galleries, which had formerly been thronged with men; while, at the same time, strong shadows were cast by the broken corridors and other ruinous parts, or fell on the ground in large masses from the lofty structure. . . . At the moment that the sun descended below the horizon, the clock in the dome of St. Peter resounded under the porticoes of Collisee. This correspondence, through the medium of religious sounds, between the two grandest monuments of Pagan and Christian Rome, caused a lively emotion in my mind. I reflected that this modern edifice would fall in its turn, like the ancient one, and that the memorials of human industry succeed each other like the men, who erected them.

Vicomte François René de Chateaubriand,
Recollections of Italy, England and America, p. 25.

1801–3

Happily for the Coliseum, the shape necessary to an amphitheatre has given it a stability of construction sufficient to resist fires, and earthquakes, and lightening [*sic*], and sieges. Its elliptical form was the hoop which bound and held it entire till barbarians rent that consolidating ring, Popes widened the breach, and time, not unassisted, continues the work of dilapidation. At this moment the hermitage is threatened with a dreadful crash, and a generation not very remote must be content, I apprehend, with the picture of this stupendous monument.

Joseph Forsyth,
Remarks on Antiquities, Arts, and Letters, p. 147.

Circa 1812

There is something in the sight of Roman monuments of antiquity that inspires the philosophic beholder with a sensation of regret, as well as of admiration. We remember that they were raised at the expense of the freedom of the rest of the world. With the exception of some of the monuments of art constructed in the earlier days of the republic, they were all erected by enslaved nations; so that the means by which they were raised must be more or less revolting to mankind in general, and some particular monuments to particular nations; as for example the Colisseum to the Jews.

John Izard Middleton,
Grecian Remains in Italy, p. 9.

1816–17

The effect of these majestick ruins is greatest when they are illuminated by the moon. Objects which time and violence have not yet mutilated, and in which we see the actual triumph of human energy over the elements lose none of their magnificence when dressed in the splendour of the sun. But the sombre twilight of the moon, gives to the aspect of desolation a melancholy expression, which speaks forcibly to the fancy and the heart. The pale and uncertain lustre which then reveals the face of things, conspires, with the silence of the hour, to aid the power of illusion, and diffuses over the objects of time past, a mysterious charm that realizes the visions of imagination.

James Sloan,
Rambles in Rome, pp. 300–301.

1817

I do remember me, that in my youth,
When I was wandering, upon such a night
I stood within the Coliseum's wall,
Midst the chief relics of Almighty Rome.
The trees which grew along the broken arches
Waved dark in the blue midnight, and the stars
Shone through the rents of ruin; and from afar
The watch-dog bay'd beyond the Tiber; and
More near from out the Caesar's palace came
The owl's long cry, and, interruptedly,
Of distant sentinals the fitful song
Begun and died upon the gentle wind.

Lord Byron,
Manfred, Scene IV.

CXXVIII

Arches on arches! as it were that Rome,
Collecting the chief trophies of her line,
Would build up all her triumphs in one dome,
Her Coliseum stands; the moonbeams shine
As 'twere its natural torches, for divine
Should be the light which streams here to illume
This long-explored but still exhaustless mine
Of contemplation; and the azure gloom
Of an Italian night, where the deep skies assume[.]

CXXIX

Hues which have words, and speak to ye of heaven,
Floats o'er this vast and wonderous monument,
and shadows forth its glory. . . .

CXLIV

But when the rising moon begins to climb
Its topmost arch, and gently pauses there;
When the stars twinkle through the loops of time
And the low night-breeze waves along the air,
The garland forest, which the gray walls wear,
Like laurels on the bald first Caesar's head;
When the light shines serene but doth not glare,
Then in this magic circle raise the dead:
Heroes have trod this spot. Tis on their dust ye tred.

Lord Byron,
Childe Harold's Pilgrimage.

The Flavian amphitheatre, emphatically named *Colossus* or *Colosseum* in the middle ages, and now *Coliseum,* is certainly one of the most extraordinary remains of antiquity that Rome still possesses,—although comparatively modern, since its erection dates only from the beginning of our aera. . . . Vespasian began the Amphitheatre in the seventy-second year of our aera, on his return from the Jewish war; and twelve thousand poor Hebrew prisoners were employed in its construction, as well as a sum of money equal to two millions of pounds sterling. The labours of the French led to the discovery of partition walls in the arena, dividing it the direction of its length into passages about twelve feet wide. . . . It is the fashion to go to the Coliseum by moonlight, as to the Vatican by torch-light; and although fashions when generally adopted become like proverbs, trite and vulgar, yet as the very currency either of a proverb or of a fashion was originally owing to some degree of merit, in respect to convenience, beauty, or wisdom; it would be more unreasonable still to abstain from doing or saying any thing, simply because it had been often done or said before, than because it never had been done or said at all. We certainly found it well worth while to go and see the Coliseum by night during a full-moon. The light played with more than usual vagueness, softness and harmony among the cavernous masses which rose in fantastic greatness on all sides of us; and such was the general appearance of the whole, that we might have fancied ourselves in the crater of an extinguished volcano rather than in any thing reared by the hand of man,—mere brick and mortar! The remaining patches of finery and all formal details had vanished; the grand ideal only remained, without a colour and almost without a shape. My notion of short-sightedness is that of perpetual moonlight, that is to say, vagueness over all distant objects: and those who are so gifted do not know how mean and poor the real world of long-sighted men is, compared with that beautifully dim one of theirs!

The Coliseum at night would be a cut-throat place but for the guard, which turns out for the protection of visitors after sun-set; and the soldiers expecting their little prequisite, are very alert. There are sentinels besides in several places among the ruins, by whom you are challenged, and the *chi viva*! the gleaming of steel, the very clatter of iron shod boots on the ancient pavement, served as picturesque touches to the scene; for imagination, like a child, feeds on empty nothings such as these.

Louis Simond,
A Tour of Italy and Sicily, pp. 167, 174, 176–77.

1817–18

Would that I could describe it to you, as it stood in its ruined loneliness amidst the deserted hills of ancient Rome. . . . The still, pale moonbeam fell on the lines of its projecting columns, range above range, to the lofty attic, in silvery light, leaving the black arches in mysterious darkness.

We passed under the great arch of entrance, passed the grass-grown area, ascended the long staircases and traversed the circling corridors. No sound met our ear but the measured tread of our own footsteps, and the whispered murmurs of our own voices. The deep solitude and silence,—the immensity and the ruin of the great fabric that surrounded us, filled our minds with awe; and as we caught the view of the stars appearing and disappearing through the opening arcades—marked the moonbeams illumining the wide range of these lofty walls, and raised our eyes to the beauty of the calm clear firmament above our head,—we could not but remember, that hundreds of ages past, these eternal lights of heaven had shown on the sloping sides of this vast amphitheatre, when they were crowded with thousands of human beings, impatient for the barbarous sports of the rising day,—where now, only the wild weeds waved as the night breeze passed over them. . . . The proud masters of the world were no more; and we . . . were wandering amidst the ruined monuments of their pride and their power, to admire their grandeur, and to mourn over their decay!

Charlotte Eaton,
Rome in the Nineteenth Century, pp. 421–22.

1818

We visited the Forum and the ruins of the Coliseum every day. The Coliseum is unlike any work of human hands I ever saw before. It is of enormous height and circuit, and the arches built of massy stones are piled on one another, and jut into the blue air, shattered into the forms of overhanging rocks. It has been changed by time into the image of an amphitheatre of rocky hills overgrown by the wild olive, the myrtle, and the fig-tree, and threaded by little paths, which wind among its ruined stairs and immeasurable galleries. . . . The interior is all ruin. I can scarcely believe that when encrusted with Dorian marble and ornamented by columns of Egyptian granite, its effect could have been so sublime and so impressive as in its present state. It is open to the sky, and it was the clear and sunny weather of the end of November in this climate when we visited it, day after day.

Percy Bysshe Shelley,
The Letters of Percy Bysshe Shelley, I, pp. 488–89.

1818

I went with Prince Metternich and his daughter, in their chariot, to the Colosseum. The moon was in her fullest splendor—the air as soft and balmy as Shakspeare's

> "Like the sweet south
> That breathes upon a bank of violets,
> Stealing and giving odour."

Two friends of the Prince who followed us, made up the only party at this scene of solitary grandeur; and the entire stillness—the melting hues of these vast masses of ruin—(for in the light they were exactly of the *same* equal force of tone with the sky, and separated only by colour and not gradation of strength)—the broad and intense depth of the shadows—the terrific loftiness of part of the fabric, which seems unsupported, and remaining because *spared* by the elements—this accumulation of impressive circumstance, together with the solemn tranquility of that interior, once resounding with the acclamations of the Roman people, at the most revolting moment of its dreadful exhibitions, but in the centre of which now stands a simple cross,—presented the most awful and sublime scene, unaccompanied by terror, that I, who am indeed but a young traveller, have ever witnessed.

Sir Thomas Lawrence, quoted in D. E. Williams,
The Life and Correspondence of Sir Thomas Lawrence, II, pp. 163–65.

1821

We have just returned from a nocturnal visit to the Colosseum, which we had been delaying for some time, till the age of the moon and the hour of her meridian should be most favourable to our purpose. This evening we set off between nine and ten, and found the sky still calm and unclouded, and the streets quiet and nearly deserted, although our way lay through some of the most populous parts of the city. . . . The arches and columns, broken and interrupted as they frequently were, also tended to perplex our way, by throwing over us alternately deep darkness and bright beams of moonlight, so that we soon began to repent our thoughtlessness in neglecting to take for a guide one of the friars who have a chapel among the ruins, and are always ready to conduct strangers.

Theodore Dwight,
A Journal of a Tour in Italy, pp. 291–92.

1823

Last night we went to see the Coliseum by moonlight, the true time for viewing it to advantage. Its vastness, its silence, and its decay, appeal most powerfully to the feelings, and when tinged by the silvery beams of the orb of night, its effect is truly sublime. . . . When we ascended to the gallery, and looked down on the arena, the moonbeams were clothing in silvery radiance one of the votive altars erected in the interior; and the large cross which crowned it was invested with a lustre that rendered it a conspicuous object, and added much to the effect of the picture. . . . To how many reflections did this visit give birth! each and all pregnant with associations of the past. The events of by-gone ages seemed unrolled before my mental vision; and there stood the cross, blessed symbol of faith! bright with the moonbeams playing over its surface, to draw my mind from gloomy cogitations of the past, to anticipations of a more cheering future.

Countess of Blessington (Marguerite Gardiner),
The Idler in Italy, II, pp. 99–101.

1829

The broken arches, upon which the seats rested, are supported by new timber and brickwork, and every passage cleared out. . . . Some spots, however, are left neglected and covered with plants and shrubs, as a sample of its former guise. My old friend [in all probability the Swiss landscapist and longtime Roman resident François Kaesermann], as an artist, is among those who regret the change; for he remembers seeing the Colosseum a beautiful wilderness of ruins, vines and shrubbery. But though the total amount is reduced, the variety, in its exposed points, and warm nooks and corners, is not less than it was; for Sebastiani, a Roman botanist, in his *Flora Colossea,* describes two hundred and sixty plants which grow there; and the number has since been found to reach three hundred.

Rembrandt Peale,
Notes on Italy, pp. 105–6.

1832

It is stupendous, yet beautiful in its destruction. From the broad arena within, it rises around you, arch above arch, broken and desolate, and mantled in many parts with the laurustinus, the acanthus, and numerous other plants and flowers, exquisite both for their color and fragrance. It looks more like a work of nature than of man; for the regularity of art is lost, in a great measure, in dilapidation, and the luxuriant herbage, clinging to its ruins as if to 'mouth its distress,' completes the illusion. Crag rises over crag, green and breezy summits mount into the sky.

Thomas Cole, quoted in Louis Legrand Noble,
The Life and Works of Thomas Cole, pp. 115–16.

1833

The clear moonlight made it almost as bright as day; every object showed itself distinctly. . . . Strange shadows fell in the moonlight upon the lofty wall; square masses of stone shot out from their regular places, and, overgrown with evergreen, looked as if they were about to fall, and were only sustained by the thick climbers. Above, in the middle gallery, people were walking, travellers, certainly, who were visiting these remarkable ruins late in the beautiful moonlight. . . . The air was of an infinitely dark blue, and tree and bush seemed as if made of the blackest velvet; every leaf breathed night. My eye followed the strangers. After they were all gone out of sight, I still saw the red glare of the torch; but this also vanished, and all around me was as still as death.

Hans Christian Andersen,
The Improvisatore, pp. 34–35.

1835

This evening I went to see the Coliseum by moonlight. It is indeed the monarch, the majesty of all ruins—there is nothing like it. All the associations of the place, too, give it the most impressive character. When you enter within this stupendous circle of ruinous walls, and arches, and grand terraces of masonry, rising one above another, you stand upon the arena of the old gladiatorial combats and Christian martyrdoms; and as you lift your eyes to the vast amphitheatre, you meet, in imagination, the eyes of a hundred thousand Romans, assembled to witness these bloody spectacles. . . . The seats have long since disappeared; and grass overgrows the spots where the pride, and power, and wealth, and beauty of Rome sat down to its barbarous entertainments. What thronging life was here then! what voices, what greetings, what hurrying footsteps up the staircases of the eighty arches of entrance! and now, as we picked our way carefully through decayed passages, or cautiously ascended some mouldering flight of steps, or stood by the lonely walls—ourselves silent, and, for a wonder, the guide silent too—there was no sound here but of the bat, and none came from without, but the roll of a distant carriage, or the convent bell, from the summit of the neighboring Esquiline. It is scarcely possible to describe the effect of moonlight upon this ruin. Through a hundred rents in the broken walls—through a hundred lonely arches, and blackened passage-ways, it streamed in, pure, bright, soft, lambent, and yet distinct and clear, as if it came there at once to reveal, and cheer, and pity the mighty desolation.

Orville Dewey,
The Old World and the New, II, pp. 80–82.

Plate #18 [old #39]

Unidentified view of a garden and religious buildings
Pen over worked-up pencil drawing, 9³/₄ x 7 inches
Neither initialed nor dated

Middleton's authorship of this drawing is questionable. Clearly not based upon a camera obscura view, its topographical value is limited and, thus, stands apart from his other drawings in the volume. The deep passages of chiaroscuro and the thick foliage of the trees, as well as the spatial imprecision, seem atypical of the South Carolinian's work. If not by Middleton, one might wonder how it came to be associated with his project and included in the volume as a proposed plate. It should be noted, however, that several views by his sketching associates had been included in Middleton's *Grecian Remains* of 1812.

1817

Of the immense space enclosed within the walls of Rome (ten or twelve square miles), much more than one half, that is nearly the whole of antique Rome, and even the convents by which it was formerly occupied, is a desert infested by malaria. . . . now their very ruins are disappearing under the luxuriant vegetation of ever-green oaks, laurels and aloes; and this residence of the masters of the world, whence as from a common centre activity was communicated to the most distant parts of the empire, seems at present the very abode of idleness. An old gardener watching his poultry, which he said were all carried away by foxes, (within the walls of Rome!) and a few beggarly-looking men employed in making ropes under the shelter of an old wall, were the only human creatures not asleep that we saw during a ramble of several hours.

Louis Simond,
A Tour of Italy and Sicily, pp. 189, 180.

1822

This part of old Rome is beautiful beyond description, and has a wild, desolate, and poetical grandeur, which affects the imagination like a dream. The very air disposes one to reverie. . . . I saw a young artist seated on a pile of ruins with his sketch-book open on his knee, and his pencil in his hand— during the whole time we were there he never changed his attitude, nor put his pencil to the paper, but remained leaning on his elbow, like one lost in extasy.

Anna Jameson,
Diary of an Ennuyée, p. 172.

PLATE #19 [OLD #20]

Porta San Paolo
1821
Camera obscura pencil tracing, 9½ x 13⁷⁄₁₆ inches
Initialed, inscribed "Roma," and dated lower right

Middleton's drawing depicts the Porta San Paolo (the old Porta Ostiensis) as seen from the Piazza San Paolo within the Aurelian Wall. The gate was constructed by the emperor Aurelian in the late third century A.D. to serve those arriving from the port of Ostia along the Via Ostiense. The gateway was rebuilt under the emperor Maxentius at the beginning of the fourth century and again a century later by Honorius. It probably was Maxentius who added the fortified courtyard arrangement with the double gateways facing the city (one of these is walled up in Middleton's view and partially concealed behind the buildings at the left). Honorius was responsible for the semicircular towers flanking the exterior of the gate. It was through the Porta San Paolo that the last Ostrogothic king, Totila, entered Rome in 549 for his second occupation of the city. Middleton's drawing shows the city side of the Porta San Paolo with its medieval additions, including the *edicola* (shrine) niche above the gate in which appears an image of Saint Peter, which replaced an earlier one of Saint Paul. Today portions of the walls to the left and right of the Porta San Paolo have been razed to accommodate the flow of traffic.

The present name of the gateway refers to the great basilican church of Saint Paul's Outside the Walls lying a short distance to the south. Middleton probably had already departed Rome when this venerable sanctuary was consumed by flames in mid July 1823. The present church represents a reconstruction begun shortly thereafter and completed in 1854.

To the right of the Porta San Paolo in this view is the 115-foot-high pyramid of the Roman praeter and tribune Caius Cestius Epulonius (d. 12 B.C.). The inspiration obviously comes from the great funereal monuments of Egypt, and this Roman pyramid attests to the expansion of republican power into the eastern Mediterranean. According to an inscription on the pyramid, its construction took but 330 days to complete. Pope Alexander VII restored the pyramid in 1663, at which time an entryway to the internal burial chamber was cut through its west side.

A bit further to the right, the Via Caio Cestio leads to the entrance of the Protestant cemetery holding, since 1738, the memorials to some four thousand principally English, German, American, and other Protestant travelers and residents in Rome, including the poets John Keats (who died in Rome in February 1821 at age twenty-five) and Percy Bysshe Shelley (who died off Spezia in July 1822 at age thirty). The importance of that burial ground for the English-speaking tourist was significant. Grace Greenwood (Sara Lippincott), for instance, put it only after the Pantheon on her itinerary of sights to be seen when she visited the city in the 1850s.

1807

"Instead [of the catacombs, says Corinne to Lord Nelvil] let us visit Cestius' pyramid. Protestants who die here are all buried around this pyramid and it is a gentler shelter, tolerant and liberal." . . . Cestius presided over the Roman games; his name is not to be found in history, but he is famous for his tomb. The massive pyramid confining him defends his death from the oblivion that has completely erased his life. Afraid that the pyramid might be used as a fortress to attack Rome, Aurelian had it surrounded by walls that still stand, not as useless ruins but as the enclosure for modern Rome.

Madame de Staël,
Corinne, p. 82.

1814–15

When I am inclined to be serious, I love to wander up and down before the tomb of Caius Cestius. The Protestant burial-ground is there; and most of the little monuments are erected to the young; young men of promise, cut off when on their travels, full of enthusiasm, full of enjoyment; brides, in the bloom of their beauty, on their first journey; or children borne from home in search of health. . . . It is a quiet and sheltered nook, covered in the winter with violets; and the Pyramid, that overshadows it, gives it a classical and singularly solemn air. You feel an interest there, a sympathy you were not prepared for. You are yourself in a foreign land; and they are for the most part your countrymen. They call upon you in your mother-tongue—in English—in words unknown to a native, known only to yourselves: and the tomb of Cestius, that old majestic pile, has this also in common with them. It is itself a stranger, among strangers. It has stood there till the language spoken round about it has changed; and the shepherd, born at the foot, can read its inscription no longer.

Samuel Rogers,
Italy: A Poem, pp. 160–61.

1817

Going out of town by the gate of St. Paolo, in order to visit the basilica of that name, about one mile in the country we saw the pyramid of Caius Cestius, a silly fellow of an ancient, who having a mind to immortalize himself, and not knowing any other way of going about it, ordered, by a clause of his will, this monument for himself; and so far succeeded, that his name has ever since remained attached to it. . . . It is curious to see how Nature, disappointed of her usual means of destruction by the pyramidal shape, goes to work in another way. That very shape affording a better hold for plants, their roots have penetrated between the stones, and acting like wedges have lifted and thrown aside large blocks, in such a manner as to threaten the disjointed assemblage with entire destruction. . . . Near at hand is the burying-ground for heretics, with a few marble monuments erected by the friends of deceased strangers. In general they are either trifling or over-fine; yet the monumental stone inscribed by a friend is more respectable than the pyramid ordered by a man's will for himself. The fate of a stranger too in a foreign land comes home to the feelings of surviving strangers, and they do not tread the sod over his grave as they would that where a citizen is interred.

Louis Simond,
A Tour of Italy and Sicily, pp. 261–62.

[Shelley's famous poetic elegy on the death of John Keats, the *Adonais*, seems in its last stanza to be strangely prescient of his own tragic death in a boating accident a little over a year later.]

1821

L

And grey walls moulder round, on which dull Time
Feeds, like slow fire upon a hoary brand;
And one keen pyramid with wedge sublime,
Pavilioning the dust of him who planned
This refuge for his memory, doth stand
Like flame transformed to marble; and beneath,
A field is spread, on which a newer band
Have pitched in Heaven's smile, their camp of death
Welcoming him we lose with scarce extinguished breath.

LV

The breath whose might I have invoked in song
Descends on me; my spirit's bark is driven,
Far from the shore, far from the trembling throng
Whose sails were never to the tempest given;
The massy earth and sphered skies are riven!
I am borne darkly, fearfully, afar:
Whilst burning through the inmost veil of Heaven,
The soul of Adonais, like a star
Beacons from the abode where the Eternal are.

Percy Bysshe Shelley,
Adonais.

Circa 1846

From one part of the city, looking out beyond the walls, a squat and stunted pyramid (the burial-place of Caius Cestius) makes an opaque triangle in the moonlight. But, to an English traveller, it serves to mark the grave of Shelley too, whose ashes lie beneath a little garden near it. Nearer still, almost within its shadow, lie the bones of Keats, 'whose name was writ in water,' that shines brightly in the landscape of a calm Italian night.

Charles Dickens,
Pictures from Italy, p. 202.

PLATE #20 [UNNUMBERED (OLD #40?)]

Unidentified view of Roman street and church apse
[The Basilica of SS. Giovanni e Paolo and the street of Clivio di Scauro
   in Rome]
1821
Camera obscura pencil tracing, 9³/₈ x 13¹/₂ inches
Initialed, incribed "Rome," and dated lower right

This and the next two views had been previously detached from their backings and were devoid of any inscriptions. Their placement in the sequence of views is problematic, but it is likely that they did fit into the intended context at this point, despite the fact that, topographically, this particular drawing would logically have come before Plate 19.

Middleton presents a view up the incline of the Caelian Hill along the ancient Clivio di Scauro as seen from the Piazza San Gregorio. The scene is dominated by the apse end of the Basilica of SS. Giovanni e Paolo and the adjacent buildings of the Passionist Monastery (occupying the site of the ancient Temple of Claudius). The church was erected upon the foundations of three ancient houses, one of which was thought to have belonged to two Christian officials martyred in 360 or 361 by the emperor Julian the Apostate; their names are commemorated by the church. The first church was constructed at the site by a Roman senator named Pammachius in the late fourth century. It subsequently was enlarged circa 499 during the reign of Pope Symmachus. Almost totally destroyed during the Norman Robert Guiscard's sack of Rome in 1084, San Giovanni e Paolo was reconstructed between 1154 and 1159 by Pope Hadrian IV (Nicholas Breakspeare, the only English pope). The apse arcade with its graceful series of fifteen small arches, constructed in the Romanesque Lombard style, may be dated from the time of Pope Honorius III (1216–27). The campanile seen to the left of the apse dates to the early twelfth century and was restored, circa 1950, with funding provided by Cardinal Spellman of New York. The supporting arches spanning the Clivio di Scauro date from the fifth to thirteenth centuries.

The Caelian Hill, one of the famed seven hills of Rome, received its name from the Etruscan king Caelius Vibenna, who, according to legend, assisted the first king of Rome, Romulus, in his war against the Sabines. According to legend, the Caelian Hill was joined to the expanding city of Rome in the seventh century B.C. when the Latian city of Alba Longa broke its peace treaty with Rome agreed upon following the combat between the Horatii and Curiatii brothers (see entries 32–34, below). In the war that ensued, the Roman king Tullus Hostilius captured Alba and removed its population to the Caelian Hill. In imperial days the Caelian was an aristocratic residential quarter; however, after the devastation wrought by the Normans in 1084, the area remained, except for its churches and monastic

institutions, sparsely inhabited, a situation evident in Middleton's view and still true today. Here one can still sense the spirit of medieval Rome and the state of relative abandonment that endured in many quarters well into the nineteenth century. The name of the street has remained essentially the same since antiquity, when it was known as the Clivius Scauri, perhaps in honor of Marcus Aemilius Scaurus, who served as consul of Rome in 115 B.C. and censor in 109 B.C.

1807

Sweet peaceful feelings took hold of Oswald when he entered the garden of San Giovanni e Paolo at sunset. . . . From there, the Colosseum can be seen, and the Forum, all the arches of triumph still standing, the obelisks, the columns. What a lovely site for such a refuge! The recluses are consoled for their nothingness as they contemplate the monuments built by those who are no longer here. From time to time, these beautiful trees cut off the view of Rome momentarily as if to double the emotion we feel in seeing it once more. It was the hour of evening when all the bells of Rome ring the *Ave Maria* . . . and the sound of brass in the distance seems to pity the dying day.

Madame de Staël,
Corinne, p. 173.

1814

This was built in the fourth century by the monk St. Pammachius, above the house of the brothers Sts. John and Paul, who were decapitated by Julian the Apostate. Several of its titular cardinals have restored it, and particularly Cardinal Fabrizio Paolucci, who rebuilt it almost completely to the designs of Antonio Canevari. Nicholas V gave it to the Gesuati, and then, when that order was suppressed, it was given to the Spanish Dominicans, and then to Mission priests, and it is now occupied by the Passionists, by order of Clement XIV.

Mariano Vasi,
A New Picture of Rome.

1817–18

The church of Santi Giovanni e Paulo, on the Caelian Mount . . . has an open gallery of small arches, supported by columns, running on the outside of the round extremity of the church; this gallery is in the round-arched style of architecture, which commenced in the decline of the Roman empire, and occurs in old churches in England.

W. A. Cadell,
A Journey in Carniola, Italy, and France, p. 323.

The streets of Rome, at no time very noisy, are for nothing more remarkable than, during the summer months, for their noontide stillness, the meridian heat being frequently so intense as to stop all business, driving everything indoors, with the proverbial exception of dogs and strangers.

Washington Allston,
Monaldi, p. 64.

PLATE #21 [UNNUMBERED (#41?)]

Unidentified scene of a wooded garden (in Rome?) with an aqueduct
and a stream
1822
Worked up pencil drawing on blue-green paper, $9^{1}/_{2}$ x $13^{1}/_{4}$ inches
Initialed and dated lower right

This finished drawing, full of romantic atmosphere, was detached from its
backing and was, thus, unnumbered in the album; it would appear, originally, to
have been the last of Middleton's views of Rome itself. It is possible that it may
have been drawn within the monastic gardens of San Giovanni e Paolo above
the Via San Paolo di Croce.

1821

XLIX
Go thou to Rome,—at once the Paradise,
The grave, the city, and the wilderness;
And where its wrecks like shattered mountains rise,
And flowering weeds, and fragrant copses dress
The bones of Desolation's nakedness
Pass, till the spirit of the spot shall lead
Thy footsteps to a slope of green access
Where, like an infant's smile, over the dead
A light of laughing flowers along the grass is spread[.]

Percy Bysshe Shelley,
Adonais.

PLATE #22 [OLD #17]

Church of the Navicella at Rome
1821
Camera obscura pencil tracing, 9³/₈ x 13¹/₄ inches
Initialed, incribed "Roma," and dated lower right

The Church of Santa Maria in Domnica (or della Navicella) is located on the Caelian Hill. The Navicella Fountain, or boat fountain, was copied for Pope Leo X (1513–22) from an ancient model. According to legend the Church of Santa Maria, with its porticoed facade, was built over the house of Saint Cyriaca, a Christian matron of the third century. The present church dates to the early ninth century and the pontificate of Saint Paschal I (817–24). The church's elegant porch was reconstructed by Andrea Sansovino after designs executed for Cardinal Giovanni de' Medici (later Pope Leo X) and attributed by some to Raphael and by others to Peruzzi.

Middleton's view of the piazza extends along the Via della Navicella to the Via Claudia. To the right is the wall enclosing the monastic property of Saint Stefano Rotondo. In the far distance, beyond the remains of the Ninfeo di Nerone, stands the Coliseum.

1800

This church is on the top of the hill, and called in Domnica, or in Ciriaca, from a religious matron, who buried the deacon St. Lawrence, and who had a house here, where she assisted and relieved the Christians in the time of the persecutions. It was consecrated and converted into a church, of which that martyr is said to have been made deacon, and to have there exercised his ministry in relieving the poor, and distributed to them, by order of Pope Sixtus, the treasures of the church. It was repaired by Pasqual I. with two much admired orders of columns of black and green granite. Leo X. rebuilt it after a design of Raphael. . . . The church is called Navicella from the small marble boat before it.

J. Salmon,
An Historical Description of Ancient and Modern Rome, I, pp. 125–26.

1817–18

The ancient church of *Santa Maria in Domnica,* called *della Navicella,* on the Caelian hill, near the Villa Mattei, is adorned with ancient columns within, and was restored, with a new front, under the direction of Raphael, by order of Leo X., who was cardinal of this church.

In the place before the church is the model of an ancient ship in marble, about fifteen feet in length. A cast of this ship, from which the place is called piazza della navicella, is to be seen in Greenwich Hospital.

W. A. Cadell,
A Journey in Carniola, Italy, and France, I, p. 322.

PLATE #23 [OLD #18]

Entrance of the Tomb of the Scipios
1821
Pencil drawing worked up over camera obscura tracing, 9⁷/₁₆ x 13⁷/₁₆ inches
Initialed, inscribed "Roma," and dated lower right

Located in the Orti degli Scipioni, just off the Appian Way, this family cemetery was discovered in 1780. The tomb was constructed in the third century B.C. within a hill of natural tufa to house the remains of Lucius Scipio Barbatus, consul in 298 B.C. and the victor over the Samnites and Lucanians; his son, a consul in 259 and the conqueror of Corsica and Algeria; Scipio Hispanis and Scipio Asiaticus, who won Spain and Asia Minor; and other members of this prominent patrician family (but not the celebrated general Scipio Africanus, who was buried an exile in Liturnium in 183 B.C.). Contrary to normal Roman burial practice of the period, the Scipio family practiced inhumation rather than cremation, and their dead, consequently, were buried in sarcophagi rather than funerary urns. Roman law forbade burials within the defined boundaries of the commune, and, although the Tomb of the Scipios lies within the Aurelian Wall that encircled imperial Rome, when it was built the tomb lay outside the Capena Gate of the old Servian Wall, which defined the official limits of republican Rome.

Today, as it has been for a number of years, the Tomb of the Scipios is closed to visitors due to its dangerous state of conservation. Removed from view, it has begun to lose the sort of memorializing quality it once had for the nineteenth-century visitor.

1817–18

On the road to the Porta San Sebastiano, a rude red-letter scrawl above the door of a vineyard, informs the passenger that this is the 'Sepolcro degli Scipioni.' We stopped and entered it, not without respect mingled with awe, at the reflection, that we were in the cemetery of a long line of republican patriots and heroes, whose unblemished name was ever ennobled by hereditary virtues and hereditary honours.

Charlotte Eaton,
Rome in the Nineteenth Century, pp. 160–61.

1818–19

Many ancient tombs may now be observed within the walls: but they were constructed before the extension of the limits by Aurelian; and at the time of their being erected, were out of the city. . . . The most ancient of these is the tomb of the Scipios, which was not discovered til 1780. . . . The tomb is in a garden, not far from the gate of S. Sebastian, to the left of the Appian road. Scarcely anything is left in it at present, the inscriptions and monuments having been carried to the Vatican and copies substituted in their room: consequently little now remains to be seen but a series of damp dark chambers by the help of a candle.

Edward Burton,
A Description of the Antiquities and Other Curiosities of Rome, I, pp. 246–47.

1819

But before I quit the mural precincts of modern Rome, my natural enthusiasm for historical antiquity will not allow me to pass over in silence the Mausoleum of the Scipios. It remained till of late unknown, though many other ruined sepulchres had been ascribed to that illustrious family. . . . But it was not till the year 1780, that chance discovered this interesting sepulchral chamber, on a little farm situated between the Via Appia and Latina. . . . Whilst enlarging the *souterains* of a casino, the labourers discovered two large tablets of peperino marble, with characters engraved and coloured with red; upon which discovery the Pope ordered the researches to be continued at his own expense for the space of a year, during which period, the magnificent sarcophagus of Scipio Barbatus, . . . was rescued from obscurity; together with many other valuable records of his illustrious family.

Richard Colt Hoare,
A Classical Tour through Italy and Sicily, II, pp. 85–86.

1820s

This Tomb is situated in a Vineyard, on the Via Appia, still nearer to the Porta S. Sebastiano than are the Baths of Caracalla: it is on the left side of the way, and the words 'Sepulchra Scipionum' are inscribed over the door. This was the Family Tomb of Lucius Cornelius Scipio Barbatus, great-grandfather of the two illustrious brothers Scipio, Asiaticus and Africanus: it is a handsome piece of architecture, very perfect, very extensive, and extremely interesting, though now robbed of its most valuable treasures, which have been removed to the Vatican Museum. The candles provided by the Custode of this Subterranean Repository, are so few in number, that persons who wish to see it distinctly, should carry lights of their own: it is excessively damp.

Mariana Starke,
Travels in Europe, pp. 162–63.

1845

Our third stoppage was at the Tomb of the Scipios. This is in a vineyard not far from the beginning of the Appian Way. We got out at the Antique Gate, a kind of portico with stone seats, and after reading the inscription—'Sepolcro dei Scipioni,' entered the Tomb. Our guide, a fine dark-eyed Italian girl in a most picturesque dress, lighted tapers, and led the way into the interior. . . . It is pleasing to muse in that quiet spot on the history of this noble race, on the many high-souled virtues which adorned, and the many stirring scenes which rendered famous the lives of some of them; and then to recall the funereal pomp and splendour which this very place has witnessed when the drama of life was closed, and the body of the great was gathered to his fathers.

Margaret Juliana Maria Dunbar,
Art and Nature under an Italian Sky, p. 183.

1847

Then the Tomb of the Scipios, through whose dark, damp, and silent chambers we passed by candle light. Oh how strange over the empty sarcophagi to read in the mouldering stone, the name of Scipio, and the date of burial. I had stood on the solitary sea-shore, where Africanus sleeps, and sighed over the fallen hero. —But here was a more familiar—a family scene, and I almost started from the close proximity of the Past. I felt like one who had ventured too far, and was becoming too familiar with awful things.

Joel T. Headley,
Letters from Italy, p. 146.

PLATE #24 [OLD #19]

Arch of Drusus at Rome modern Porta San Sebastiano
1821
Pencil drawing worked up over camera obscura tracing, 9¹/₂ x 13¹/₂ inches
Initialed, inscribed "Roma," and dated lower right

Once thought to have been a triumphal arch erected in the first century B.C. in honor of Augustus's stepson Drusus, it is more likely to have been a framed archway of an elevated aqueduct allowing for the passage of the roadway. Its present appellation was, in fact, not given to the arch until the sixteenth century. The aqueduct, the Acqua Antoniniana, was one of Rome's last and served the nearby Baths of Caracalla of the third century. The arch originally had three openings, of which only the one remains. The external face is flanked by two columns of *giallo antico* (purplish-red streaked marble) with composite capitals.

On this spot the Roman senate and people received a triumphal procession into the city when Marcantonio Colonna II was accorded the honor for his role in the victory over the Turks at Lepanto in 1571.

The Aurelian Wall and the Porta San Sebastiano are shown beyond the Arch of Drusus. Originally the Porta San Sebastiano was known as the Porta Appia. It was rebuilt by the emperors Honorius and Arcadius in 401–2, at which time the flanking towers were added. The Porta San Sebastiano was restored yet again by the Byzantine generals Belisarius and Narses in the sixth century. Beyond the Aurelian Wall the famous tomb-lined stretch of the Appian Way begins and can be followed past the church of Domine Quo Vadis (where Christ is supposed to have appeared to Saint Peter), several of Rome's most famous catacombs, the Circus of Maxentius, and the impressive Tomb of Cecilia Metella. The Appian Way, along which we look in Middleton's drawing, was opened in 312 B.C. under the magistracy of Appius Claudius Caecus. It led from the old Capena Gate in the Servian Wall into the Campagna region to the south and eventually across the Apennine Mountains to the Adriatic port of Brindisi. Of the many great roads of Roman antiquity, the Via Appia is, perhaps, the most celebrated.

1817–18

Within the Porta San Sebastiano is the arch of Drusus. Over this arch there passed an aqueduct, a branch of the Aqua Marcia. This arch is built of large blocks of Travertine. Each of the two stones forming the key of the arch is about nine feet long. There is no ancient inscription on the arch by which its original destination might be ascertained, but it is supposed by Venuti [*Descrisione delle Antichita di Roma*, 1763] to be the arch mentioned by Tacitus built in honour of Nero Claudius Drusus; and according to Venuti, Caracalla afterwards made use of this arch for the passage of the aqueduct or branch which he added to the Aqua Marcia.

W. A. Cadell,
A Journey in Carniola, Italy, and France, I, p. 494.

PLATE #25 [OLD #21]

Tomb of Cecilia Metella near Rome
1821
Camera obscura pencil tracing, $9^7/_{16}$ x $13^7/_{16}$ inches
Initialed, inscribed "Roma," and dated lower right

Located at the third milestone along the old Appian Way leading south from the Porta San Sebastiano at the crest of a hill, the Tomb of Cecilia Metella is one of the most important monuments along the road. The marble-faced drum is 65 feet, 7 inches in diameter and rises from a square concrete base. It follows the tumulus traditions of the Etruscans and serves as a precedent for both the tomb of Augustus, of slightly later date, and the Mausoleum of Hadrian, the present-day Castel Sant' Angelo. It is colloquially called the Capo di Bove, a name inspired by the liturgical frieze of ox skulls encircling it.

Cecilia Metella was the daughter of Quintus Metellus Creticus and the daughter-in-law of the triumvir M. Licinius Crassus, one of Caesar's generals in Gaul. Pope Boniface VIII gave the tomb to his Caetani family relatives in 1300 to use as a fortress. They erected a rectangular fortification to enclose the road. The tomb, now capped with crenellations, served as the castle's keep. Toll was exacted from all the travelers going to and from Rome along the Via Appia. In disgust, traffic began to bypass the castle, eventually creating a new roadway, called the Via Appia Nuova, which entered the city through the Porta San Giovanni. The old stretch of the Via Appia eventually fell into disuse. The abandonment helped to preserve the many Roman tombs lining the ancient road until they could be archaeologically excavated and conserved in the nineteenth century.

1817

CANTO IV
There is a stern round tower of other days,
Firm as a fortress, with its fence of stone,
Such as an army's baffled strength delays,
Standing with half its battlements alone,
And with two thousand years of ivy grown,
The garland of eternity, where wave
The green leaves over all by time o'erthrown;—
What was this tower of strength? Within its cave
What treasure lay so lock'd, so hid?—A woman's grave.

Lord Byron,
Childe Harold's Pilgrimage.

1817

This morning we rode out of the walls of the city to the tomb of Cecilia Metella, the wife of Crassus the Triumvir. This beautiful sepulchral monument is situated on a slight eminence, at the side of the Appian-way. The material of which it is built is a light brown stone, the form of it is circular, and, under the frieze of an elegant entablature, a wreath of festoons and oxen's heads runs around it. Battlemented walls were raised on the top of the tomb, in the middle ages, by the Gaetani family, and this peaceful abode of the dead was converted into a place of tumult and blood. The sarcophagus of Greek marble which was found within is removed to the Farnese palace, and nothing is now to be seen but an empty cone, fallen in at the top, and fringed around with shrubs and vines. From the wonderful thickness and great simplicity of the structure, it is surprising that it presents so few marks of age and decay. It is connected with the ruins of an old castle, ivy creeps over both, weeds and brambles grow out of the crevices, and hang over the walls, and the whole has an air of solitude and desolation.

Rev. William Berrian,
Travels in France and Italy, pp. 135–36.

1826–28

We will quit these pleasant dales, and ride across the fields, a short mile, to the line of ruined tombs that marks the remains of the Appian Way. An extensive pile of ruins will naturally first attract our attention; and we will spur our horses up the sharp acclivity on which it stands, though making a small detour, and getting into the rough road, that still leads out on the old route for a few miles, we might reach the summit more easily. On reaching this spot, we find the remains of a castle of the middle ages, with courts, walls, and towers, scattered about the fields, all built in the usual rude and inartificial manner of those structures, with a keep, however, that has the grace and finish of Roman architecture. . . . The walls of this keep are thirty feet thick, the interior being little more than a small vaulted room. It formerly contained the sarcophagus that is still seen in the court of the Farnese Palace; for, in brief, this keep was merely one of the tombs of the Appian Way! . . . It is the tomb of Caecilia Metella, the wife of a mere triumvir, a millionnaire of his day. . . . It is probably the noblest mausoleum now standing in Europe.

James Fenimore Cooper,
Gleanings from Europe, p. 206.

About two miles, or more, from the city-gate, and right upon the roadside, Kenyon passed an immense round pile, sepulchral in its original purposes, like those already mentioned. It was built of great blocks of hewn stone, on a vast, square foundation of rough agglomerated material, such as composes the mass of all the other ruinous tombs. But whatever might be the cause, it was in far better state of preservation than they. On its broad summit rose the battlements of a medieval fortress, out of the midst of which (so long since had time begun to crumble the supplemental structure, and cover it with soil, by means of wayside dust) grew trees, bushes, and thick festoons of ivy. This tomb of a woman had become the citadel and donjon-keep of a castle; and now all the care that Cecilia Metella's husband could bestow, to secure endless peace for her beloved relics, had only sufficed to make that handful of precious ashes the nucleus of battles, long ages after her death.

Nathaniel Hawthorne,
The Marble Faun, II, pp. 233–34.

PLATE #26 [OLD #22]

Papal Palace at Castel Gandolfo
1822
Pencil drawing worked up over camera obscura tracing, 9½ x 13½ inches
Initialed and dated lower right

This and the next thirteen of Middleton's views depict scenes of the "Castelli Romani," the romantic Latian hill towns in the volcanic mountain district lying just to the southeast of Rome. A visit to the Alban Hills and adjoining crater lakes of Albano and Nemi was almost an imperative for all nineteenth-century visitors to the Roman region.

Castel Gandolfo, perched above the crater lake of Albano, is named after the twelfth-century Gandolfi family of Genoa. The castle passed to the Savelli family and then to the Vatican in 1596. Since 1604 it has been an integral part of the papal property and the longtime summer residence of the papacy. The pontifical palace incorporates parts of the old castle but was rebuilt between 1624 and 1629 by Carlo Maderno for Pope Urban VIII and later was enlarged by Alexander VII (1655–67), Clement XIII (1758–69), and Pius IX (1846–78). In addition to its long line of papal residents, Castel Gandolfo has hosted Goethe, the classical scholar Johann Winckelmann, Angelica Kaufmann, and Massimo d'Azeglio, the Italian artist and statesman, who lived here at the time of Middleton's visit.

Although there is no physical evidence to date the town earlier than the eleventh century, Castel Gandolfo supposedly occupies the site of the ancient town of Alba Longa, founded, according to legend, in 1152 B.C. by Ascanius, the son of Aeneas. Thus Alba Longa was held to be the mother of Rome. The celebrated *mano-a-mano* combat between the Curiatii and the Horatii took place near here in the war between Rome and Alba Longa during the time of Roman king Tullus Hostilius (672–40 B.C.).

1817

About a mile from Albano, is Castel Gandolfo, a small village. It was near there that Milo, going to Lavinium, the place of his birth, was attacked by Clodius, who was killed in the contest. It was made the subject of a fine harangue by Cicero. Here also is the Lake of Albano, which was the crater of a volcano, and is eight miles in circumference.

Henry Sass,
A *Journey to Rome and Naples,* p. 130.

1818

A charming road shaded with fine trees brought us the next day to Castel Gandolfo. We did not stop to see either the interior of the palace or the gardens, which we understood are uninteresting; but we visited the Barberini gardens near it, which are well planted and enjoy a fine prospect.

Louis Simond,
A *Tour of Italy and Sicily,* p. 312.

PLATE #27 [OLD #23]

Castel Gandolfo, Soracte in the Distance
1822
Camera obscura pencil tracing, 9½ x 13½ inches
Initialed and dated lower right

The domed church within the town is that of San Tomaso da Villanova, built for Pope Alexander VII by Bernini in 1661. Sketchily indicated in the distance can be made out the height of Monte Soracte some 35 miles away, up the Tiber Valley north of Rome. Such a far-sighted view can seldom be glimpsed today due to the general haze that now hangs over the sprawling Roman city.

1817

Still following the horizon towards the north along the snowy ridge of the Apennine, Mount Soracte rears its high insulated cone over the plain of Etruria, separated by the Tiber from the country which the Romans called Latium Novum.

Louis Simond,
A Tour of Italy and Sicily, p. 165.

1819–20

To the left appear the heights of Castel Gandolfo, swelling above the infected plain, the only remnant of beauty and salubrity in this once lovely paradise. Upon this spot, Power and the Church have seized; and the Pope's Villa, (a vast palace,) with a cluster of religious edifices, crown its summits and command the lake; on whose beautiful shores the Franciscans have raised a convent, precisely on the spot where the antique village of Alba Longa was placed, ere it was destroyed by the Romans under Tullus Hostilius.

Lady Sydney Morgan,
Italy, p. 265.

1843

A path leads down from the town to the shores of the lake, which swarm with frogs in the summer. The lake of Albano, one of the most beautiful pieces of water in the world, and, in respect to scenery, beyond comparison the finest of those of purely volcanic origin in Italy. . . .

John Murray,
Murray's Handbook of Rome and Its Environs, p. 387.

PLATE #28 [OLD #24]

Nymphaeum on the Lake of Albano
1822
Pencil drawing, 9⁹/₁₆ x 13½ inches
Initialed and dated lower right

The nymphaeum may be that of the villa of the Roman emperor Domitian near Castel Gandolfo. The scene in Middleton's drawing may also possibly be connected with the Ninfeo Bergantino, built by Domitian inside an abandoned quarry near the entrance to the Emissarium, constructed by the Romans to drain water from Lago Albano and celebrated in Virgil's *Aeneid*. A similar drawing is preserved among the artist's works at Middleton Place Plantation.

1817–18

Not far from hence [the Emissarium], along the shore of the lake, are some artificial caves, or grottos, hollowed out in its rocky precipitous banks, called, by the country people, the Bagni di Diana, or Grotto delle Ninfe, and supposed to be the remains of a Nymphaeum built by Domitian.

A soft green sward, spotted with magnificent trees, gently slopes to the margin of the water; luxuriant ivy, hanging in wreaths nearly to the ground, shades its mouth, and a multitude of plants mingle their green pensile foliage from the rocks above. The natural grandeur of this immense cavern, the vaulted roof, the lofty arches, and 'long withdrawing' recesses, partially seen within the deep shade of its interior, . . . the woody height of Monte Cava towering into the bright blue heavens, and reflected in the crystal mirror of the lake; the verdure and stillness, and seclusion that breathe around, form one of the most enchanting scenes I ever beheld.

As the grottos of this lake, however, form the only undoubted remains of an ancient Nymphaeum now left in the world, I shall give you a particular account of them. The entrance of the principal grotto is a wide and lofty arch of fine Roman brickwork, through which the sun-beams, playing amidst waving wreaths of ivy, break beautifully on the caverned roof. . . .

Charlotte Eaton,
Rome in the Nineteenth Century, III, pp. 375–77.

1818

The immediate borders of the lake are praised for their beauty; yet notwithstanding the abruptness of the banks, they are in many places marshy, overgrown with reeds twenty or thirty feet high, and the haunt of reptiles in a deleterious atmosphere. The ascending landscape seen over-head athwart the blue sky, is however very fine. At the water-side there are artificial grottoes (*Nymphaea*), partly hollowed into the mountainside and partly built on a strange plan with many niches for statues, and secret passages, and recesses for baths.

Louis Simond,
A Tour of Italy and Sicily, p. 313.

PLATE #29 [OLD #25]

Emissarium on the Lake of Albano
1822
Camera obscura pencil tracing, 9½ x 13½ inches
Initialed and dated lower right

The Emissarium tunnel is described in the works of Livy (V, 15), Dionysius (XII, 8), and Plutarch ("Life of Camillus," 3). According to tradition, it was cut in 397 B.C. to satisfy the predictions of an oracle about a prerequisite to the Roman taking of the Etruscan city of Veii. The tunnel actually dates from a later time, but it does illustrate the cuniculus tradition of hydraulic engineering inherited by the Romans from their Etruscan neighbors. The tunnel is one and a half miles long, averaging four feet wide and five feet high, and is cut through a solid volcanic deposit of peperino and basalt. It is located just to the east of Castel Gandolfo. Middleton represented the lakeside entrance of the Emissarium as plate 10 of his *Grecian Remains*.

1817

The canal from this lake [Albano] is one of the most ancient and singular works of the Romans. . . . From this [lake] they began to pierce the mountain; so that, at the end of a year, they had made a canal a mile long, three feet and a half wide, and six feet high. This work, cut through the rock with blows of the hammer and chisel, cost immense sums. It was made with so much solidity, that it is still used, without ever having had any reparation.

Henry Sass,
A Journey to Rome and Naples, pp. 130–31.

1818

The descent from the top of the bank of the Albano lake down to its waters was rather steep; but travellers of any spirit will not miss the opportunity of viewing one of the oldest monuments of Roman ingenuity and perseverance,—the celebrated *emissario*. It is a tunnel nearly two miles in length, forming now the only outlet to the waters of the lake, which otherwise would fill the hollow of the crater till it ran over, four hundred feet above this artificial channel. The entrance, three feet and half wide and six feet high, is solidly built of large hewn stones, arched at top; and by means of a lighted candle sent down the stream floating on a piece of wood, you discover the same construction carried on as far as sight can reach.

Louis Simond,
A Tour of Italy and Sicily, pp. 312–13.

PLATE #30 [OLD #26]

From the Convent of Capucines at Albano
1822
Pencil drawing worked up in part over camera obscura tracing,
  9$\frac{1}{2}$ x 13$\frac{1}{2}$ inches
Initialed and dated lower right

A similar scene showing one of the chapels of the stations of the cross was depicted by Middleton in the *Grecian Remains* and titled "View from the Grotto of the Convent of the Capuchins at Albano." The scene recorded here is at the end of the Galleria di Sopra road, which runs along the lip of the crater lake of Albano. Here the road branches, one track leading to Ariccia, another to Albano Laziale, and a third to the Palazzola.

1817–18

After breakfast . . . we mounted our asses, which carried us all with great ease and safety, although the long legs of some of the gentlemen nearly touched the ground. We passed the Capuchin Convent, the terrace of which,—forbidden to females,—commands a most beautiful prospect, and then turning along the banks of the lake, wound through magnificent woods and thick copses of oak, chestnut, and hazel, looking down into the deep crystal basin below, and above to the towering summit of the classic mountain whose sylvan sides we were ascending. . . . Amidst the trees appeared a rustic chapel to the Madonna.

Charlotte Eaton,
Rome in the Nineteenth Century, III, pp. 383–84.

1834–35

That part of the road which looks down upon the lake passes through a magnificent gallery of thick embowering trees, whose dense and luxuriant foliage completely shuts out the noonday sun. . . . This long sylvan arcade is called the *Galleria-di-sopra,* to distinguish it from the *Galleria-di-sotto,* a similar, though less beautiful avenue, leading from Castel Gandolfo to Albano, under the brow of the hill. In this upper gallery, almost hidden amid its old and leafy trees, stands a Capuchin convent, with a little esplanade in front, from which the eye enjoys a beautiful view of the lake and the swelling hills beyond. It is a lovely spot,—so lonely, cool, and still, and was my favorite and most frequented haunt.

Henry Wadsworth Longfellow,
Outre-Mer, p. 259.

135

PLATE #31 [OLD #27]

Ancient Tomb within Rock at Pallazuola Site of Alba Longa
1822
Camera obscura pencil drawing worked up in upper portions,
    13¹/₂ x 9¹/₂ inches
Initialed and dated lower right

This repeats the view published as plate 4 in Middleton's *Grecian Remains* and is the only such replication in the later series of drawings. The Palazzola, from the Latin *Palatiolis* (or little palace), was a villa of ancient origin having been constructed circa 125 B.C. by members of the Roman Scipio Hispanus family. Abandoned in the fourth century A.D., it was reoccupied in 1025 by members of the Benedictine Order, who built a church and a monastery from the ruins. Subsequently, the property came under the auspices of both Augustinian and Cistercian monks. Still later it served as a country retreat of the Colonna family with a Carthusian monastery appended to it. In 1460 members of the Franciscan Friars Minor made it their home. In Middleton's day the Palazzola was in the hands of Portuguese Franciscans who had embarked upon an energetic rebuilding campaign in the previous century. The Palazzola later (1920) became the summer residence of the English College, which continues to use it for retreats and conferences.

Immediately adjacent to the monastic buildings of the Palazzola is this strange cliff-face tomb decorated with lictors' fasces on either side of a bisellium with its priestly cap and staff. The combination of secular and religious symbols in a funereal monument might point to the tomb as the resting place of Cn. Cornelius Scipio Hispallus, who was both pontiff and consul in the year 176 B.C. and who died after presiding over festivities on the Alban mount. The tomb had attracted the attention of visitors long before Middleton's day. When Pope Pius II Piccolomini made an antiquarian tour of the area in 1463, he noted: "To the right very high precipices fall to the lake, to the left is a towering cliff in which the ancients hewed out a path with iron tools. At the left before you enter the monastery there is a high wall-like rock on which according to ancient custom were sculptured the fasces of a Roman consul and twelve axes. Six were covered with ivy, six were still visible. Pius ordered the ivy to be cleared away to encourage the memory of antiquity." The tomb was later depicted by Piranesi in his *Antichita d'Albano*. The clarity of the carving has deteriorated markedly since Middleton's visit, and the garden from which he viewed it is now a chicken yard.

Circa 1812

In the garden of the convent at Pallazuola is a very singular and ancient tomb, sculptured in the solid rock. There are various conjectures concerning it. Some suppose it to be the sepulchre of a consul, Cn. Cornelius, whom Livy (l. 41. c.16) mentions to have fallen sick, after having sacrificed at the Mons Albanus, and to have died at Cumae. His body was transported to Rome, where he had a magnificent funeral; and 'chi sa,' says the abbate G. Antonio Ricci, 'che non fosse riposto in questo sepolcro!' (*Mem. Stor. del Citta de Alba.*) This negative mode of arguing is a very singular one for an antiquary. 'Chi sa che fosse' is the natural answer. Others conjecture that it was the tomb of Tullius Hostilius. This is far more probable, as he scarcely would have been buried at the place he took pleasure in destroying.

I am inclined to think it of still greater antiquity, and to be a monument of some Alban king. The fasces and eagle would prove only that those insignia were borrowed by the Romans from the Albans; indeed with some little variation, as on examination it will be observed that these fasces are in some degree different from those of Rome.

John Izard Middleton,
Grecian Remains in Italy, p. 22.

1817–18

In a monastary at Palazzuolo, near Albano, is the tomb with twelve fasces cut on the rock. It is unknown to whose memory it was erected.

W. A. Cadell,
A *Journey in Carniola, Italy, and France*, I, p. 445.

1817–18

To the left appear the heights of Castel Gandolfo, swelling above the infected plain, the only remnant of beauty and salubrity in this once lovely paradise. Upon this spot, Power and the Church have seized; and the Pope's Villa, (a vast palace,) with a cluster of religious edifices, crown its summits and command the lake; on whose beautiful shores the Franciscans have raised a convent, precisely on the spot where the antique village of Alba Longa was placed, ere it was destroyed by the Romans under Tullus Hostilius.

Charlotte Eaton,
Rome in the Nineteenth Century, III, pp. 384–85.

1843

Palazzola, a Franciscan monastery, beautifully situated at the foot of Monte Cavo, overlooking the lake of Albano. . . . The garden of the monastery is remarkable for a consular tomb. It is excavated in the rock, and is supposed to be as old as the 2nd Punic war. It was first discovered in 1463 by Pius II . . . who had it cleared of the ivy which had concealed it for ages. It was not completely excavated until 1576, when considerable treasure is said to have been found in the interior. The style of the monument closely resembles that of the Etruscan sepulchres—a fact which bespeaks its high antiquity, independently of the consular fasces and the emblems of the pontiff sculptured on the rock. . . . This tomb must have stood on the side of the road that led from the Via Appia to the Via Numinis and Temple of Jupiter, on the Monte Cavo above.

John Murray,
Murray's Handbook of Rome and Its Environs, p. 383.

PLATE #32 [OLD #28]

Tomb at Albano Vulgo of the Horatii & Curatii
1822
Camera obscura pencil tracing, 9½ x 13½ inches
Initialed and dated lower right

Most commonly called the Tomb of the Horatii and Curiatii, this ancient sepulchre recalls the legendary combat between three Roman brothers and three Alban brothers to settle a longstanding conflict between the two cities. According to the story, the initial encounter saw two of the Horatii brothers of Rome slain and the three Alban Curiatii brothers wounded. Cleverly feigning flight, the remaining Horatii brother managed to separate the injured Curiatii brothers and fight each of them separately to the death. The city of Alba then surrendered peaceably to Roman control. The number of cones atop the base of the tomb probably accounts for the association with this legend.

The tomb was described as early as 1463 by Pope Pius II Piccolomini during his visit to the Castelli Romani:

> In the part looking toward Ariccia is to be seen a square pile despoiled of its outer wall, on the summit of which rise five lofty pyramids. Three are stripped of the hewn stone with which they were once faced while two still retain their ornament. Time, the foe of all things, has so shaken some of the stones that they threaten to fall and in many places it has allowed the foe of walls, the wild fig tree, to wedge itself in. This is popularly called the tomb of the Curiatii, who fought with the three Roman Horatii in defense of their liberty and fell in the battle. They say that two pyramids were added for the two Horatii who fell at the same time.

The tomb has also been called the Tomb of Aruns (son of the great Etruscan king Lars Porsenna), but this name is probably of later republican date. The base is forty-six feet square and the height is twenty-three feet. The base is composed of square blocks of peperino surmounted by one central and two corner cones; originally the other two corners were crowned in similar fashion.

Charlotte Eaton (*Rome in the Nineteenth Century,* III, pp. 380–81) notes that several theories circulated in her day concerning its original function: that it was the tomb of the Horatii and Curiatii; that it was the Tomb of Pompey the Great; that it was the mausoleum of Pompey's family who had their family seat at nearby Alba; and that it was a cenotaph to Pompey with the five pyramids commemorating the five victories he won in his first consulship.

The tomb was drawn by Antonio da Sangallo and Peruzzi in the sixteenth century and was engraved by both Piranesi and Rossini in the eighteenth century. The monument was stabilized subsequent to Middleton's visit in 1825 by Giuseppe Valadier. The Church of Santa Maria della Stella is shown beyond the tomb. This former Carmelite monastery is built above several Christian catacombs containing a number of early frescoes. Two years after Middleton's visit, the bodies of two local martyrs, Innocent and Felix, were discovered here.

PLATE #33 [OLD #29]

Same Tomb
1822
Camera obscura pencil tracing, 9½ x 13⅝ inches
Initialed and dated lower right

1805

We left Velletri this morning in a heavy storm of rain; we passed thro the little town of Riccia founded by Archelous Siculus 500 years before the Trojan war and called Hermina—from hence we proceeded to Albano. Just before we entered this town we passed to the right a high sepulchral monument originally adorned with five cones or pyramids three or four of which are still standing. This is said to be the Tomb of the Curiatii.

Washington Irving,
The Complete Works of Washington Irving,
I, pp. 260–61.

1826–28

Albano . . . is in the region so long contested in the early wars of Rome; and the celebrated battle of the Horatii is thought to have been fought here. A tomb is still standing, though a ruin, near the town, which, it is pretended, was erected in honour of them; but then the tomb of Ascanius is also shown!

James Fenimore Cooper,
Gleanings from Europe, p. 187.

1833

We changed horses at the pretty village of Albano, and, on leaving it, passed an ancient mausoleum, believed to be the tomb of the Curiatii who fought the Horatii on the spot. It is a large structure, and had originally four pyramids on the corners, two of which only remain.

Nathaniel Parker Willis,
Pencillings by the Way, p. 56.

1834–35

But my chief delight was in sauntering along the many woodland walks, which diverge in every direction from the gates of La Riccia. One of these plunges down the steep declivity of the hill, and threading its way through a most romantic valley leads to the shapeless tomb of the Horatii and the pleasant village of Albano.

Henry Wadsworth Longfellow,
Outre-Mer, p. 258.

PLATE #34 [OLD #30]

Same Tomb
1822
Pencil drawing worked up over camera obscura tracing, 9½ x 13½ inches
Initialed and dated lower right

Circa 1812

Here immediately before the church, and in the centre of the Appian way, which divides and winds round it, stands a very uncouth and extraordinary monument, formed of a square basis, and five conic towers thence vulgarly called the tomb of the Horatii and Curiatii. This conjecture is certainly false, as we have the authority of Livy (Lib. i. 25) for their having been buried in different places. He says, the sepulchres existed at his time on the spots where each of them separately fell. . . . Nevertheless, the family of the Savelli took care to propagate the error, by erecting an inscription, purporting that it was the tomb of the Horatii. This is luckily now fallen. The most accredited conjecture is, that it is the tomb of Pompey, and that the five towers, of which three are now fallen, alluded to his five victories, for which he obtained triumphs: this is the opinion of Ligorius; and we find in Plutarch, that the remains of Pompey were brought and deposited at Albano.

John Izard Middleton,
Grecian Remains in Italy, pp. 19–20.

1848

We have scarcely had two hours without rain since we came [to Albano]. . . . Today we have not been out, but I have paddled to Aruns' tomb, Porsena's son, who was killed in their attack upon Aricia during the retreat from Rome—a great ugly Etruscan thing with five ruined cones.

Florence Nightingale,
Florence Nightingale in Rome, pp. 277, 279–80.

PLATE #35 [OLD #31]

On the [illegible] *Near Albano*
1822
Pencil drawing worked up over camera obscura tracing, $9^3/_8$ x $13^3/_8$ inches
Initialed and dated lower right

This rustic and romantic structure lying somewhere along the short stretch of road between Albano and Ariccia has not been located.

1820s

The air, both at Albano and Aricia (one mile distant), is less oppressive during summer, though perhaps not more salubrious, than at Rome: and the country is beautiful. Private lodging-houses may be procured at each place; and a public carriage goes three times a week, during summer, from Rome to Albano; the fare, for going, being five pauls, and the same for returning.

Mariana Starke,
Travels in Europe, p. 234.

PLATE #36 [OLD #32]

Same cottage
1822
Pencil drawing worked up over camera obscura tracing, $9^5/_8$ x $8^3/_8$ inches
Initialed and dated lower right

PLATE #37 [OLD #33]

Prince Chigi's palace at L'Aricia
1822
Pen over camera obscura pencil tracing, $8^3/_{16}$ x $12^1/_4$ inches
Initialed and dated lower right

Middleton's viewpoint in this drawing of the hill town of Ariccia is from the Vallariccia ravine on the old road from Albano to Ariccia. Ariccia was an ancient Latin town figuring in stories of Rome's early warfare with her southern hill-town neighbors and was the traditional site of a decisive battle in the fifth century B.C. in which a confederation of Latin tribes and Greeks defeated an Etruscan army led by Aruns, the son of the celebrated Lars Porsenna. The Etruscan loss assured their eventual withdrawal from the area south of the Tiber and the independence of Rome. In Cicero's day Ariccia became a *municipium*.

During the Middle Ages, Ariccia was a possession of the Counts of Tusculum before passing to the Savelli, who sold it to the Chigi of Siena in 1661. Palazzo Chigi with its four square corner towers was restored in 1664 by Bernini for Pope Alexander VII. The domed church of Santa Maria dell'Assunzione dates to 1662–64 and was one of Bernini's most significant commissions.

Ariccia and this particular view of the approach to the town were very popular with artists. Prosper Barbot, a friend of the French painter Jean-Baptiste-Camille Corot, wrote that he found there "a numerous company of landscapists of all countries: four compatriots, plus Italians, Germans, English, Russian." Views of Ariccia were plentiful among the Americans as well; examples exist by George Inness, Russell Smith, Jasper Cropsey, George Loring Brown, Robert Weir, and Sandford Gifford. Visitors, however, had to exercise caution when traveling about the area in Middleton's day, since the environs were infested with brigands.

Today the romantic road through the Vallariccia ravine has lost both its original function and its charm. The modern road connecting Albano with Ariccia now passes high overhead across a viaduct constructed between 1847 and 1854, in its day an engineering marvel and still an impressive monument to mid-nineteenth-century technology.

1818

From Albano to Velletri, the scene is continually varied with woody dells and rocky heights. On the top of one of the latter, La Riccia is perched up in a most beautiful situation; but some of our friends who were lodging there, scarcely ventured to stray out of sight of the gates of the little town, for fear of being carried off [by bandits].

Louis Simond,
A Tour of Italy and Sicily, p. 388.

1829

I passed the month of September at the village of La Riccia, which stands upon the western declivity of the Albanian hills, looking towards Rome. Its situation is one of the most beautiful which Italy can boast. Like a mural crown, it encircles the brow of a romantic hill; woodlands of the most luxuriant foliage whisper around it; above rise the rugged summits of the Abruzzi, and beneath lies the level floor of the Campagna, blotted with ruined tombs, and marked with broken but magnificent aqueducts that point the way to Rome. The whole region is classic ground. . . .

The town itself, however, is mean and dirty. The only inhabitable part is near the northern gate, where the two streets of the village meet. There face to face, upon a square terrace, paved with large, flat stones, stand the Chigi palace and the village church with a dome and portico. There, too, stands the village inn, with its beds of cool, elastic maize-husks, its little dormitories, six feet square, and its spacious saloon, upon whose walls the melancholy story of Hippolytus is told in gorgeous frescos. And there, too, at the union of the streets . . . rises the wedge-shaped Casa Antonini, within whose dusty chambers I passed the month of my *villeggiatura*. . . .

My daily occupations in this delightful spot were such as an idle man usually whiles away his time withal in such a rural residence. I read Italian poetry, strolled in the Chigi park, rambled about the wooded environs of the village, took an airing on a jackass, threw stones into the Alban Lake, and, being seized at intervals with the artist-mania, that came upon me like an intermittent fever, sketched—or thought I did—the trunk of a hollow tree, or the spire of a distant church, or a fountain in the shade.

Henry Wadsworth Longfellow,
Outre-Mer, pp. 255–56.

1829

During the summer months, La Riccia is a favorite resort of foreign artists who are pursuing their studies in the churches and galleries of Rome. Tired of copying the works of art, they go forth to copy works of nature; and you will find them perched on their campstools at every picturesque point of view, with white umbrellas to shield them from the sun, and paint-boxes upon their knees, sketching with busy hands the smiling features of the landscape.

Henry Wadsworth Longfellow,
Outre-Mer, p. 354.

1833

From Albano we were to go [to Genzano] on foot for the short and beautiful remainder of the way through Ariccia. Resida and golden cistus grew wild by the roadside, thick, juicy olive trees cast a delicious shade; I caught a glimpse of the distant sea, and upon the mountain slopes by the wayside, where a cross stood, merry girls skipped dancing past us, but yet never forgetting piously to kiss the holy cross. The lofty dome of the church of Ariccia I imagined to be that of St. Peter, which the angels had hung up in the blue sky among the olive trees. In the street, the people had collected around a bear which danced upon his hind-legs, while the peasant who held the rope blew upon a bagpipe the selfsame air which he had played at Christmas, as Pifferari, before the Madonna. . . . I was quite willing to stop there instead of going onto Genzano.

Hans Christian Andersen,
The Improvisatore, pp. 20–21.

PLATE #38 [OLD #34]

L'aricia
1822
Pen over camera obscura pencil tracing, $9^7/_{16}$ x $13^7/_{16}$ inches
Initialed and dated lower right

1828–29

ARICCIA

Sikul built the town, it's been thousands of years and its citizens
Asked Latium's king in the neighboring grove for council.
Your woods are cool and the air is healthy and you boast yourself
therefore to the English to now be a summering place.

Wilhelm Waiblinger,
Werke und Briefe, I, p. 358.

PLATE #39 [OLD #35]

Church near L'aricia
1822
Pen over camera obscura pencil tracing, $9^1/_2$ x $13^3/_8$ inches
Initialed and dated lower right

1828

> [Ariccia] is a very delightful spot—situated on a gentle hill, surrounded for miles with beautiful forest scenery . . . and the interchange of hill and vale—of woodland and cultivated fields, reminds me more of New England than anything I have seen on the continent.
>
> Henry Wadsworth Longfellow,
Letters of Henry Wadsworth Longfellow, I, p. 274.

PLATE #40 [OLD #36]

Ardea—in Latium
1822
Camera obscura pencil tracing, $9^{1}/_{2}$ x $13^{1}/_{2}$ inches
Initialed and dated lower right

Ardea is a Latian town in the coastal region south of Rome situated on the Via Laurentina. It is reputed to have been founded by the legendary Perseus and, later, to have been the ancient capital of Turnus, king of the Rutuli and adversary of the Latin people. Ardea, reportedly, never fell to Roman might but was absorbed into the widening sphere of Roman influence, retaining a measure of independence and its prosperity into the imperial period. The town remained prosperous during the Middle Ages, passing into the hands of a branch of the powerful Colonna family in the early fifteenth century and to the Cesarini family in 1564. Ardea, like so many other communities in the Roman Campagna, felt the onslaught of malaria, and its population dwindled. John Murray reported the inhabitants of the town in 1864 as numbering only one hundred, and Robert Burn in 1871 noted that "the present village occupies only a small part of the ancient site, and numbers about 200 inhabitants" (*Rome and the Campagna*, p. 369).

Middleton's view shows, on the right, the twelfth-century fortress rebuilt atop the ancient acropolis in the fifteenth century as the Palazzo Colonna-Sforza Cesarini (much damaged in World War II); the twelfth- to thirteenth-century church of San Pietro is on the left.

1800

This noble town is twenty miles from Rome, and three from the sea, called also Troja. Pliny is of the opinion, that it was built by Danae, mother of Perseus; Dionysius [of Halicarnassus] traces its origin from a son of Ulysses and Circe, and says it was named from the augury of the bird Ardea. According to Ovid however it was burnt by Aeneas for having opposed his enterprises, from whom perhaps it derived its last appellation; and the road towards Rome, celebrated in the Acts of the Martyrs, was called Ardeatina. Of this city, when resplendent with the royal residence of the Rutuli, Pliny informs us there were in the temple of Juno some fine ancient pictures, among which was one of Marcus Ludius, held in great estimation. Till the time of Gelasius II. [1118–19] it continued powerful, when this pope, pursued by Henry IV. retreated here, before he retired to Gaeta, his native place.

J. Salmon,
An Historical Description of Ancient and Modern Rome, II, pp. 300–301.

159

PLATE #41 [OLD #37]

Ardea
1822
Camera obscura pencil tracing, 9¼ x 13½ inches
Initialed and dated lower right

Ardea also suffered drastically from wartime destruction. It lay in the path of the Allied advance from the Beachhead at Anzio and was heavily damaged in May 1944. Much of what Middleton depicted in this and the previous view, including the town's fortifications and the Cesarini Castle, has either been obliterated or reduced to ruin. Ardea's primary attraction today is the splendid museum dedicated to the sculptures and paintings of the Italian twentieth-century artist Manzu, who, for a number of years, maintained his studio here.

1820s

Another road goes from Antium [the modern Anzio] in the opposite direction. . . . This road, though rough, is practicable for carriages; and the drive occupies about three hours: the magnificent forest-scenery embellishes this road; but as a considerable part of it traverses very thick woods, where tracks of the wheels of charcoal-carts cross each other in every direction, it is necessary to take a well-experienced Guide . . . to point out the way to Ardea. . . . A considerable portion of the walls of the Citadel of Ardea . . . is still in existence; and a few modern cottages, a church, and a baronial castle of the lower ages, which last now belongs to the Cesarini family, occupy the site of the ancient fortress. The entrance to the modern village is through a Gateway, apparently constructed during the lower ages. Among the cottages, in the village still dignified by the name of Ardea, is a Wine-House where bacon, hams, and macaroni are sold; and where Travellers who bring their own dinner may have it cooked by their own servants or by the owner of the wine-house: and the Cesarini family, if a proper application be made to them, will give their agent at Ardea an order to provide Travellers with an eating-room and beds in the Villa Cesarini.

Mariana Starke,
Travels in Europe, pp. 237–38.

1843

Ardea occupies the crest of a lofty rock, distant 4 m. from the sea, and insulated by deep natural ravines except at one point, where it is united to the table-land by an isthmus. . . . The approach to the gate and the appearance of the rock from all parts of the plain is exceedingly picturesque, but malaria is so severe in summer that the village is almost deserted. . . . There is a small wine-shop at Ardea where travellers may obtain refreshment; but the best plan will be to obtain an order from the Cesarini family at Rome, which will procure accommodation in their castle.

John Murray,
Murray's Handbook of Rome and Its Environs, p. 439.

PLATE #42 [OLD #38]

Tomb on the Tiber
1820s
Camera obscura pencil tracing, 8½ x 12 inches
Neither initialed nor dated

Based upon a comparison with a landscape drawing by Theodore Wilkins (Thomas Ashby Collection in the Vatican Library) dated 1716, which shows the Tiber valley near Acqua Acetosa, Middleton's tomb could be the Torre Lazzaroni, although it also might be identified with a number of other towers originally constructed in 814 in defense of the area by Pope Leo IV. Several of these towers were set upon actual Roman tombs. If this association is correct, Middleton could have done the drawing on the same occasion in 1822 when he sketched the Ponte Milvio and the fountain at Acqua Acetosa. One might compare this building with that in Claude Lorrain's *Mill on the Tiber* of circa 1650, now in the Nelson-Atkins Museum of Art in Kansas City.

1821

From the Gate of the People we travelled some time along the ancient Via Flaminia, the stones of which are built into the walls of vineyards on both sides. . . . Here and there were the ruins of old square towers and battlemented walls, which served to remind us of the barbarism which had flowed into Italy with the Goths and Vandels, and to make us melancholy at the thoughts that we had left the ancient seat of the arts, and were bound to a country once so prolific in uncivilized nations.

Theodore Dwight,
A Journal of a Tour in Italy, pp. 345–46.

PLATE #43 [OLD #42]

Unidentified coastal view, perhaps of the Harbor of Genoa,
    with a cross-topped column and resting travelers
1820
Camera obscura pencil tracing, worked up with some use of ink
    at lower left and right, 7¼ x 9⅞ inches
Initialed and dated lower right

This is the earliest dated drawing in the Middleton album. It was detached from its backing and, thus, is unnumbered and without identifying inscription. Some faint pencil writing can be seen on the reverse, perhaps reading "Grand aux de la Toile."

1818

From hence quite to Sestri, the Apennines extend into the sea with rugged precipices, so that, instead of beholding the ocean from a sandy beach, you stand upon the brink of the mountain, and look off upon the waste of waters which flow up almost to the point perpendicularly below your feet. At the distance of every few leagues, as the mountains run off in spurs, you have deep ravines to cross, where the roads are so narrow and steep, that the mule makes his way with caution and difficulty. . . . but whether on the sides or summits, you are still on the brink of the sea, and have a boundless prospect over the Mediterranean, and of the innumerable vessels which coast along these shores. . . . We had upon this journey, one of the most beautiful sunsets I ever enjoyed. We descended from the higher regions into a beautiful narrow vale, through which the road lay to the seaside, where we came upon the Bay of Sestri. Here is a noble promontory to the south; a peninsula, the extreme point of which is finely covered with wood, and a smooth curved beach, with a noble back-ground of mountains. The scene was enlivened by the great number of little boats, with the fishermen just landing, on their return to their families, after the toils of the day. . . . The next day we had a noble prospect of 'the *magnificent*' Genoa from the summit of Recco.

Matthias Bruen,
Essays, Descriptive and Moral, pp. 102–3, 107–8.

1821

In an instant a turn in the path brought us round the obstructing rocks; and with great surprise and pleasure we gazed on the Mediterranean, which lay stretched out almost too far for the eye to follow it, until it met the sky. . . . As we proceeded with a prospect now open, now obstructed, we gradually gained the highest point of the whole road—a bare ridge which overlooked the neighboring mountains. . . . On the left lay the ocean, at a depth below which we despaired of estimating, stretching out to the west till it almost touched the sun.

Theodore Dwight,
A Journal of a Tour in Italy, pp. 439–40.

PLATE #44

Bagni di Lucca
1821
Camera obscura pencil drawing, worked up in part, 9½ x 13½ inches
Initialed "J. I. M. Lucca" and dated lower right

This drawing depicts one of the most famous Italian medicinal spa areas of Middleton's day. In this view we look down the Lima stream to the southwest toward its confluence with the Serchio. Beyond the houses, inns, and apothecary shops lining the banks of the Lima is the historic bridge of the Ponte a Serraglio, supposedly constructed in 1317 by the lord of Lucca, Castruccio Castracane.

Tradition traces the use of the thermal springs, collectively called the Bagni di Lucca, back to the days of Julius Caesar, but they were first documented in 1245 when they were visited by Emperor Frederick II. Among later users were Dante, various members of the great Medici family of Florence, two popes, the sixteenth-century French philosopher Michel de Montaigne, and the exiled James of England. During the Napoleonic era Elise Bonaparte, the princess of Lucca, had her summer residence at the baths. Among her summertime guests was the court musician of Lucca, the virtuoso violinist Niccolò Paganini. Following the end of Napoleonic rule in Lucca, the baths continued to be used as the principality's summer capital by their Bourbon successors, who entertained Count von Metternich, the distinguished Austrian politician, there in 1817.

Correspondence preserved in the South Carolina Historical Society in Charleston mentions a stay of Mrs. Eliza Middleton in Lucca in 1821. Apparently John Izard Middleton accompanied his wife to the baths while she sought relief from the medical problems with which she was afflicted. By the time of Middleton's visit, the baths had attracted a host of foreign pilgrims; in fact, by the end of the nineteenth century a sizable English-speaking colony had been established at the Bagni di Lucca, which even tolerated an active Anglican church. Throughout the nineteenth century the healing waters of these baths were sampled by such literary figures as Heinrich Heine, Lord Byron, Victor Hugo, Percy Bysshe Shelley and his wife Mary Wollstonecraft Shelley (of *Frankenstein* fame), Alfred Tennyson, Robert and Elizabeth Browning, and John Ruskin. The Americans Mark Twain, William Wetmore Story, and Marion Crawford also were among the celebrated visitors—Crawford, in fact, having been born at the Bagni di Lucca in 1854.

1802

The village of *Dei Bagni* stands in the bottom of a valley, on the banks of the Serchio; the baths themselves, with the lodging houses round them, are on the declivity of the hill. The view from thence extends over a dell deep, broken, and shagged with trees; a torrent rolling over a rocky bottom; the hills all clad in forests of chestnut; at a distance and above all the pyramidal summits of the *cloud-capped Apenines*. The baths are indeed in the very heart of these mountains, but surrounded rather with the beautiful than the grand features of their scenery. These baths do not appear to be a place of gay fashionable resort, or likely to furnish much social amusement; but such persons as retire for purposes of health or improvement, may find here tolerable accommodations, and a country to the highest degree picturesque and interesting.

Rev. John Chetwode Eustace,
A Classical Tour through Italy, II, p. 276.

1818

In a few days we leave for the Bagni di Lucca, a kind of watering-place situated in the depth of the Apennines; the scenery surrounding the village is very fine. . . . We shall see something of Italian society at the Bagni di Lucca, where the most fashionable people resort.

Percy Bysshe Shelley,
The Letters of Percy Bysshe Shelley, II, p. 468.

1828

The dwellings at the baths of Lucca are situated either below, in a village surrounded by high hills, or are placed on one of these hills, which is not far from the principal spring, where a picturesque group of houses peeps down into the charming dale. But many are scattered here and there on the sides of the hill, and are attainable only by a wearisome climb through a wild paradise of vines, myrtle bushes, honeysuckles, laurels, oleanders, geraniums, and similar high-born plants. I have never seen a lovelier valley, particularly when one looks from the terrace of the upper bath; where the solemn green cypresses stand; down into the village. We there see a bridge bending over a stream called the Lima, which cuts the village in two. At its either end there are waterfalls leaping over rocky fragments with a roar, as though they would fain utter the pleasantest things, but could not express themselves distinctly on account of the roaring echo.

The great charm of the valley is owing to the circumstance that it is neither too great nor too small, that the soul of the beholder is not forcibly elevated, but rather calmly and gradually inspired with the glorious view; that the summits of the mountains themselves, true to their Apennine nature, are not magnificently misshapen in extravagant Gothic form, like rocky caricatures, just as the men in German lands on them are human caricatures; but so that their nobly rounded, cheerful green forms seem of themselves inspired with the civilization of art, and accord melodiously with the blue heaven.

Heinrich Heine,
Pictures of Travel, II, pp. 136–37.

I fully expect that, in a few years, this attractive spot will become one of the largest water-ing places in Europe. . . . for, beside the pleasant circle of the English, you may be sure of meeting, from time to time, intelligent people of all lands; . . . for do not the intelligent people of all lands visit Italy? . . . and do not all visitors to Italy. . . . or, at least, a good many of them . . . come to revive themselves at the Baths of Lucca?

Mrs. Trollope,
A Visit to Italy, I, pp. 347, 349.

PLATE #45 [OLD #43]

Chapel Near the Hot Baths of Lucca
1821
Camera obscura pencil drawing, worked up in part, 9½ x 13½ inches
Initialed "J. I. M. Lucca" and dated lower right

The little chapel represented in Middleton's drawing has not been specifically identified, but the Bagni Caldi (hot baths) at the Bagni di Lucca are well known. The Bagni Caldi (also known as the Bagni di Corsena), themselves, were among the oldest of the seven thermal stations in the area, having been the one visited by Emperor Frederick II. By Middleton's day the spa would have looked much as it does now; the bath building fronts onto a trapezoidal piazza flanked by substantial buildings, several of which formed the villa of Maria Antonietta, the wife of Grand Duke Leopold II of Tuscany (1824–59), and a casino constructed by Elise Bonaparte between 1805 and 1814. The chapel was probably located a bit higher up the mountain slope.

1818

These thermal springs have the high temperature of 60° Reaumur (160° Fahrenheit), and are much frequented. The road to them, by its peculiar smoothness, reminded us of that along the western side of Loch Lomond. We have spent two days in exploring a very fine country. One of our rambles carried us to the *Prato Fiorito* on the top of a mountain which cannot well be less than six or seven thousand feet high, since we found snow remaining in various places. The extensive pastures well deserved the name they bear, and would have done no discredit to Switzerland; the views from them were varied and magnificent. . . . After the dusty roads, the pickpockets, and the cut-throats of Southern Italy, it is really delightful to enjoy the verdure, fresh air, and security of these mountains.

Louis Simond,
A Tour of Italy and Sicily, p. 575.

1841

I cannot express to you one half the pleasure I feel, at finding myself here. . . . I had no idea that any spot so abounding in its shade, so sheltered from the scorching sun, so freshened by the eternal coolness of a briskly-running stream. . . . could have been found in July, on this side of the Alps. . . . and the shade too, is not the thin straggling shade of olive-trees, but that of chestnut, beech, and oak. . . . It is perfect enchantment!

Mrs. Trollope,
A Visit to Italy, I, p. 294.

PLATE #46 [OLD #45]

Arch of Augustus near Susa
28 April 1823
Camera obscura pencil tracing, 12½ x 9½ inches
Initialed and dated lower right

This is the first of three drawings in Middleton's series that he dated with both day and month as well as year. The date and location would indicate that it was executed while on a return trip across the Alps to France.

The town of Susa is located in the Piedmont region of Italy west of Turin at an Alpine crossing into France commanding the roads to Mont Cenis and Montgenèvre. The Mont Cenis road was the most direct route between France and Italy, leading from Paris through Lyons and Chambery across the pass and down to Susa and Turin.

The Arch of Augustus, on the Via degli Archi, was erected in honor of Rome's first emperor by Cottius in 8 B.C. Cottius was the king of the Alobroges, a tribe allied to Rome, in whose hands Augustus left the Mont Cenis route across the Alps supported by a detachment of Roman troops based in Susa (the ancient Segusium). The arch's frieze commemorates the conclusion of the federal agreement between the Roman emperor and his vassal.

1817

Suza is the first city in Piedmont [coming from Savoy]. Tradition tells us that Hercules passed here to penetrate into Gaul; that it was by this place also that Hannibal effected his entrance into Italy. There is a triumphal arch in honour of Augustus, which still preserves the beautiful proportions and taste of Roman architecture.

Henry Sass,
A Journey to Rome and Naples, pp. 67–68.

1818

Near Susa, on an old Roman road which seems to have followed the course of the Dora Riparia over the Alps, and which intersects nearly at right angles the modern road by Mount Cenis, stands a triumphal arch dedicated to Augustus in the year 745 of Rome, by the people of Suza. . . . This arch, built of large blocks of marble in a good style of architecture, formerly bore several inscriptions in gilt bronze fastened on with lead, which were torn off by the French, as we were told on the spot. It might not be by them; but the report serves to show how well established is their reputation for plundering even among their friends, for the people here were not by any means averse to French dominion.

Louis Simond,
A Tour of Italy and Sicily, p. 610.

173

PLATE #47 [OLD #46]

(Bon Place Charmotte) near Chambery
2 May 1823
Camera obscura pencil tracing, 8 x 9³/₄ inches
Initialed and dated lower right

This estate is located in the Savoy/Rhone-Alps district of southwestern France. Chambery was the old capital (1232–1562) of the duchy of Savoy, which, as part of the Kingdom of Sardinia, preserved its independence until 1860, when its territory was divided among France, Italy, and Switzerland. The little villa of Les Charmettes was the home of Louise de Warens, the patroness and lover of the Swiss-French philosopher and political theorist Jean-Jacques Rousseau (1712–78). She was a widow when they met and he but sixteen years old and fifteen years Madame de Warens's junior. Rousseau lived at Les Charmettes from 1730 to 1742 before moving to Paris, where he was to begin those works that would ensure his reputation as one of the greatest thinkers of the Enlightenment.

Middleton might have had a special fondness for Rousseau and a familiarity with his writings through his own association with Madame de Staël. Staël had published her *Lettres sur Jean-Jacques Rousseau* in 1788. The work was translated into English a year later and was republished in 1820.

1820–22

> We proceeded to Les Charmettes, up a steep ascent, not very safe or easy for a carriage, along a shady glen, with sloping cultivated fields on each side; and to the left of the road is a rivulet which murmurs in its rocky channel, forming several little waterfalls in its descent. . . . The house and garden are at a little distance from the road to the right. . . . A French gentleman was waiting at the house for the keys of the upper apartments, which are rarely shown to strangers. After some delay and difficulty, the keys were sent. The lower rooms are nearly unfurnished. In the parlour, there is a miserable portrait of Rousseau, representing him as a very old man, with the Contrat Social in his hand. . . . The chamber of Madame de Warrens [*sic*] is up stairs, facing the garden, and out of it is a small room fitted up as a chapel or oratory. The room formerly occupied by Rousseau is over the front door.
>
> From the upper windows we had a fine view over the distant country, illumined by the crimson glow of the setting sun, which blending with the reflection of the deep azure of the sky, spread a flood of purple light over the mountains. . . . Under a climate like this, amid the grandest and most beautiful scenery, we need not wonder that the ardent and intensely susceptible mind of young Jean Jacques caught the inspiration and enthusiasm, which breathe through all his descriptions of nature.
>
> R. Bakewell,
> *Travels*, I, pp. 157–60.

175

PLATE #48

Entrance of Les Charmotte
2 May 1823
Camera obscura pencil tracing, 10 x 14¼ inches
Initialed and dated lower right

1817

Early this morning, we took a guide to the Charmettes, the too famous retreat of Madame De Warens. It is really most beautiful, and answering strictly Rousseau's description. . . . Rousseau does not say enough of the rivulet, which runs along a hollow way, covered over with trees, with here and there a very fine glimpse of the prospect between the branches; he does not say enough of the *petit bois de châtaigniers,* which hangs down the slope, where the house is built: it is very small; two rooms and a kitchen below (the kitchen a late addition), and three bedrooms upstairs; the stone stairs very wide and massy. Madame de Warens' room and Rousseau's were adjoining. The garden is of course odious; the *vigne* above, and the *verger* below, scarcely less so.

Louis Simond,
Switzerland; or, A Journal of a Tour and Residence in that Country, pp. 235–36.

1820–22

On the front of the house is an inscription, placed there by Herault Desechelles, when he was commissioner from the [French Revolutionary] Convention in 1792. The poetry has nothing to recommend it; but it gives a tolerably correct picture of the extraordinary character who once resided there.

> Réduit, par Jean Jacques habité,
>
> Tu me rappelles son génie,
>
> Sa solitude, sa fierté,
>
> Et ses malheurs et sa folie.
>
> A la glorie, à la vérité,
>
> Il osa consacrer sa vie,
>
> Et fut toujours persecuté,
>
> Ou par lui-même, ou par l'envie.

'Retreat, inhabited by Jean Jacques, thou recallest to my mind his genius; his solitude; his pride; his folly, and his misfortunes. He dared to consecrate his life to truth and glory; and was always persecuted either by himself or by envy.'

R. Bakewell,
Travels, I, p. 161.

PLATE #49 [OLD #47]

Voltaire's Chateau at Ferney
1823
Camera obscura pencil tracing, 9¼ x 13¾ inches
Initialed and dated lower right

The Ferney estate of the great French philosopher Voltaire (François Marie Arouet [1694–1778]) is located four miles from Geneva, Switzerland, in France. The chateau was bought for Voltaire by Marie-Louise Mignot, the widow of Nicolas-Charles Denis. The philosopher lived there between 1758 and 1778, and it was there that he wrote his novels *Candide* and *Irène* and the *Dictionnaire philosophique*, as well as his histories of Russia under Peter the Great, the age of Louis XV, and the *Essai sur l'histoire générale et sur les moeurs et l'esprit des nations.*

1817

Five miles north of Geneva, and two miles from the lake, is the chateau of Fernex, pronounced Ferney, once the residence of Voltaire. It is a neat country house, of moderate size, beautifully situated, with the Jura hills to the north. The proprietor said he was annoyed by the visits of the curious, and with some difficulty granted permission to see the salon and bed-room, which are hung with prints and pictures, and furnished as when Voltaire lived. The bed-curtains are almost entirely gone, his admirers having taken away shreds of them to keep as relics.

W. A. Cadell,
A Journey in Carniola, Italy, and France, II, p. 206.

1818

The chateau of Ferney, the celebrated residence of Voltaire, six miles from Geneva, is a place of very little picturesque beauty, notwithstanding the Alps and the Jura; its broad front is turned to the high road, without any regard to the prospect, and the garden is adorned with cut trees, parapet walls with flower-pots, jets d'eaux, etc. Voltaire's bedroom is shewn in its pristine state, just as he left it in 1777, when, after a residence of twenty years, he went to Paris to enjoy a short triumph, and die. Time and travellers have much impaired the furniture of light-blue silk, and the Austrians, quartered in the house three years ago, have not improved it; the bed-curtains especially, which for the last forty years have supplied each traveller with a precious little bit, hastily torn off, are of course in tatters; the house-keeper indeed is so well aware of this, that she purposely turns away, to afford you the opportunity for the poetical theft, expecting her fees to be the more liberal on that account. The bed-stead is of common deal, coarsely put together; a miserable portrait of Le Kain, in crayons, hangs inside of the bed, and two others, equally bad, on each side, Frederic, and Voltaire himself. Round the room are bad prints of Washington, Franklin, Sir Isaac Newton, and several other celebrated personages; the

ante-chamber is decorated with naked figures, in bad taste; each of the two rooms may be twelve feet by fifteen. . . . Very few remain alive of those who saw the poet; a gardener who conducted us about the grounds had that advantage. . . . The old gardener spoke favourably of his old master, who was, he said, *bon homme tout à fait, bien charitable,* and took an airing every morning in his coach and four.

Louis Simond,

Switzerland; or a Journal of a Tour and Residence in that Country, I, pp. 393–94.

1822

Went to Ferney to-day—that Ferney, where Voltaire constantly occupied *by,* and *for,* the world which he affected to despise, spent so considerable a portion of his time. The *salon,* and *chambre à coucher,* are preserved in the same state as when he inhabited them; except that the curtains of his bed have suffered from the desire visitors have evinced to possess a small portion of them. . . . I confess it gave me pleasure to obtain a few relics at Ferney; and among the rest, a portion of that curtain, beneath whose shade a head so often reposed, whose cognitations have been disseminated over all of Europe. . . . The garden and pleasure grounds at Ferney, have nothing remarkable; except it be a trellissed walk, planned by Voltaire, with openings like windows in the sides, to admit views of the fine scenery around. This was his favorite promenade, and he sauntered for hours in it, with a note-book, in which he entered his reflections. . . . A garrulous old gardener, who acted as our cicerone, had lived with, and professed to remember the philosopher perfectly. He described him as vivacious and irascible to a degree, violent while the irritation continued, but placable and kind when it had subsided. . . . The gardener remembered to have one day observed an English traveller approach close to the terrace where Voltaire was standing, and stare at him with an air of intense curiosity. Voltaire turned himself round and round, that the stranger might have a more distinct view of him; then retired and desired his secretary to demand *dix sous* from the stranger for having seen the lion.

Countess of Blessington (Marguerite Gardiner),
The Idler in Italy, I, pp. 41–43.

Voltaire lived just under the Jura, on a hillside, overlooking Geneva and the lake, with a landscape before him in the foreground that a painter could not improve, and Mont Blanc and its neighbor mountains the breaks to his horizon. At six miles off, Geneva looks very beautifully, astride the exit of the Rhone from the lake; and the lake itself looks more like a broad river, with its edges of verdure and its outer-frame of mountains. We walked up an avenue to a large old villa, embosomed in trees, where an old gardener appeared, to show us the grounds. We said the proper thing under the tree planted by the philosopher; fell in love with the view from twenty points; met an English lady in one of the arbours, the wife of a French nobleman to whom the house belongs, and were bowed into the hall by the old man, and handed over to his daughter to be shown the curiosities of the interior. There were Voltaire's rooms, just as he left them. . . . It is a snug little dormitory, opening with one window to the west; and, to those who admire the character of the once illustrious occupant, a place for very tangible musing. They showed us afterwards his walking-stick, a pair of silk stockings he had half-worn, and a night-cap. The last article is getting quite fashionable as a relic of genius.

Nathaniel Parker Willis,
Pencillings by the Way, pp. 390–91.

Bibliography

Adams, Henry. *The Education of Henry Adams.* Boston, 1918.

Allston, Washington. *Monaldi and "The Angel and the Nightingale."* 1841. Reprint, ed. Nathalia Wright. Delmar, N.Y.: Scholars' Facsimiles & Reprints, 1991.

Amfitheatrof, Erik. *The Enchanted Ground: Americans in Italy, 1760–1980.* Boston and Toronto: Little, Brown & Co., 1980.

Amory, Martha Babcock. *The Wedding Journey of Charles and Martha Babcock Amory . . . 1833–1834.* Boston, 1922.

Andersen, Hans Christian. *The Improvisatore, or Life in Italy.* Trans. Mary Howitt. London: Richard Bentley, 1847.

————. *A Poet's Bazaar.* Trans. Charles Beckwith. 3 vols. London, 1846.

Anonymous. "Original Letters, from an American Traveller in Europe to his Friends in this Country," *Monthly Anthology* (January–December 1807, January–December 1808, January–August 1809).

————. "Review of Bonstettin's *Voyage*," *American Review* 4 (July 1812): 121.

————. "A Walk about Rome," *Southern Literary Messenger* 9 (March 1843): 175.

The Arcadian Landscape: Nineteenth-Century American Painters in Italy. Lawrence: University of Kansas Museum of Art, 1972.

Armstrong, Sir Walter. *Lawrence.* London: Methuen, 1913.

Ashby, Thomas. *The Roman Campagna in Classical Times.* Ed. J. B. Ward-Perkins. London: Ernest Benn / New York: Barnes & Noble, 1970.

Bagnani, Gilbert. *The Roman Campagna and Its Treasures.* New York: Charles Scribner's Sons, 1930.

Bailey, Brigitte Gabke. "Pictures of Italy: American Aesthetic Response and the Development of the 19th-Century American Travel Sketch." Ph.D. diss., Harvard University, 1985. Ann Arbor: University Microfilms, 1986.

Baker, Paul R. *The Fortunate Pilgrims: Americans in Italy, 1800–1860.* Cambridge: Harvard University Press, 1964.

Bakewell, R. *Travels Comprising Observations Made during a Residence in the Tarentine, and Various Parts of the Grecian and Pennine Alps, and in Switzerland and Avergne, in the Years 1820, 1821, and 1822.* Vol. I. London: Longman, Hurst, Rees, Orme and Brown, 1823.

Bancroft, George. *Poems.* Cambridge: Harvard University Press, 1823.

Bell, John. *Observations on Italy.* Edinburgh and London: William Blackwood/ T. Cadell, 1825.

Berrian, Rev. William. *Travels in France and Italy in 1817 and 1818.* New York: I. & S. Sword, 1821.

Biddle, Edward, and Mantle Fielding. *The Life and Works of Thomas Sully (1783–1872).* Charleston, S.C.: Garnier, 1964.

Blessington, Countess of (Marguerite Gardiner). *The Idler in Italy: Journal of a Tour.* 2 vols. Philadelphia: Carey & Hart, 1839.

Bober, Phyllis Pray, and Ruth Rubenstein. *Renaissance Artists and Antique Sculpture: A Handbook of Sources.* London: Harvey Miller/Oxford: Oxford University Press, 1986.

Bonaventura, Arnaldo. *I Bagni di Lucca, Coreglia, e Barga.* Bergamo: Istituto italiano d'arti grafiche, 1914.

Bonstettin, Karl Victor von. *Reise in die klassischen Gegenden Roms.* Leipzig: J. F. Kartknoch, 1805.

———. *Voyage sur la scène des six derniers livres del'Eneide.* Ed. Michel Dentan. 1805. Rpt. Lausanne: Bibliothèque romande, 1971.

British School at Rome. *Thomas Ashby: un archeologo fotografa la campagna romana tra '800 e '900.* Rome: De Luca, 1986.

Brooks, Van Wyck. *The Dream of Arcadia: American Writers and Artists in Italy, 1760–1915.* New York: E. P. Dutton, 1958.

———. *The World of Washington Irving.* New York: E. P. Dutton, 1944.

Broughton, Lord (John Cam Hobhouse). *Italy: Remarks Made in Several Visits from the Year 1816 to 1854.* 2 vols. London: John Murray, 1859.

Bruen, Matthias. *Essays, Descriptive and Moral; On Scenes in Italy, Switzerland, and France by an American.* Edinburgh: Archibald Constable, 1823.

Bryant, William Cullen. *Letters of a Traveller or Notes of Things Seen in Europe and America.* New York: G. P. Putnam, 1850.

Bull, Duncan. *Classic Ground: British Artists and the Landscape of Italy, 1740–1830.* New Haven: Yale Center for British Art, 1981.

Burn, Robert. *Rome and the Campagna: An Historical and Topographical Description of the Site, Buildings, and Neighbourhood of Ancient Rome.* Cambridge: Deighton, Bell & Co. / London: Bell and Daldy, 1871.

Burton, Edward. *A Description of the Antiquities and Other Curiosities of Rome: from Personal Observation during a Visit to Italy in the Years 1818–19.* 2 vols. London: C. & J. Rivington, 1828.

Butler, William Allen. *A Retrospect of Forty Years.* Ed. Harriet Allen Butler. New York: Charles Scribner's Sons, 1911.

Byron, Lord (George Gordon). *Childe Harold's Pilgrimage and Other Romantic Poems*. Ed. John D. Jump. London: J. M. Dent, 1975.

Cadell, W. A. *A Journey in Carniola, Italy, and France in the Years 1817, 1818*. 2 vols. Edinburgh: Archibald Constable, 1820.

Carter, Nathaniel Hazeltine. *Letters from Europe*. vol. 2. New York: Cavill, 1827.

Channing, William Ellery. *Conversations in Rome: Between an Artist, a Catholic, and a Critic*. Boston: Crosby & Nichols, 1847.

Chateaubriand, Vicomte François René de. *Recollections of Italy, England and America*. Philadelphia: M. Carey, 1816.

Clark, John A. *Glimpses of the Old World*. Philadelphia, 1840.

Clark, Kenneth. *Landscape into Art*. Boston, 1961.

Coffey, John W. *Twilight of Arcadia: American Landscape Painters in Rome, 1830–1880*. Brunswick, Maine: Bowdoin College Museum of Art, 1987.

Cogswell, Joseph. *Life of Joseph Green Cogswell as Sketched in His Letters*. Ed. Anna Eliot Tichnor. Cambridge, Mass., 1874.

Cole, Thomas. *Notes at Naples*. 1832.

———. *Thomas Cole's Poetry*. Ed. Marshall Tymn. York, Pa.: Liberty Cap Books, 1972.

Cooper, James Fenimore. *Excursions in Italy*. 2 vols. Paris, 1838.

———. *Gleanings from Europe: Rome*. Ed. John Conron and Constance Ayers Denne. Albany: State University of New York Press, 1981.

Cox, Samuel S. *A Buckeye Abroad*. New York, 1852.

Dewey, Orville. *The Old World and the New, or, A Journal of Reflections and Observations Made on a Tour in Europe*. 2 vols. New York: Harper & Brothers, 1836.

Dickens, Charles. *Pictures from Italy*. 1846. Reprint, ed. David Paroissien. New York: Coward, McCann & Geoghegan, 1974.

Di Macco, Michela. *Il Colosseo: funzione simbolica, storica, urbana*. Rome: Bulzoni, 1971.

Dinnerstein, Lois. "The Significance of the Colosseum in the First Century of American Art." *Arts Magazine* 58 (1984): 116–20.

Dodwell, Edward. *Views and Descriptions of Cyclopian, or, Pelasgic Remains in Greece and Italy; with Constructions of a Later Period from Drawings by the Late Edward Dodwell*. London: Adolphus Richter, 1834.

Dunbar, Margaret Juliana Maria. *Art and Nature under an Italian Sky*. London: Thomas Nelson & Sons, 1860.

Dunlap, William. *A History of the Rise and Progress of the Arts of Design in the United States*. 3 vols. New York: Dover, 1969.

Dwight, Theodore. *A Journal of a Tour in Italy in the Year 1821, with a Description of Gibralter by an American*. New York: Abraham Paul, 1824.

Earnest, Ernest. *Expatriates and Patriots: American Artists, Scholars, and Writers in Europe*. Durham: Duke University Press, 1968.

Eaton, Charlotte A. *Rome in the Nineteenth Century*. Edinburgh: Constable, 1820.

Eldredge, Charles, and Barbara Novak. *The Arcadian Landscape: Nineteenth-Century American Painters in Italy*. Lawrence: University of Kansas Museum of Art, 1972.

Emerson, Ralph Waldo. *Journals of Ralph Waldo Emerson*. Ed. Edward Waldo Emerson and Waldo Emerson Forbes. London: Constable, 1910.

————. *The Letters of Ralph Waldo Emerson*. Ed. Ralph L. Rusk. New York: Columbia University Press, 1939.

Eustace, Rev. John Chetwode. *A Classical Tour through Italy in 1802*. London: J. Mawman, 1815.

————. *A Tour through Italy, Exhibiting a View of Its Scenery, Antiquities, and Monuments, Particularly as They are Objects of Classical Interest*. 2 vols. Philadelphia: M. Carey, 1816.

Evans, Grose. *Benjamin West and the Taste of His Times*. Carbondale: Southern Illinois University Press, 1959.

Farley, John. *Over Seas in Early Days*. Ed. Joseph Pearson Farley. Kansas City, 1907.

Fay, Theodore Sedgwick. *Norman Leslie*. Vol. 2. New York, 1835.

Fisher, Joshua Francis. "Excerpts from a Memoir of Joshua Francis Fisher (1807–1873)." In *The Diary of Harriet Manigault, 1813–1816*, 137–45. Rockland, Maine, 1976.

Fisk, Wilbur. *Travels in Europe*. New York: Harper, 1843.

Forsyth, Joseph. *Remarks on Antiquities, Arts, and Letters during an Excursion in Italy, in the Years 1802 and 1803*. London: John Murray, 1835.

Freeman, James Edward. *Gatherings from an Artist's Portfolio*. New York: Appleton, 1877.

Fuller, Margaret, Marchioness Ossoli. *At Home and Abroad or Things and Thoughts in America and Europe*. Ed. Arthur B. Fuller. 1856. Port Washington, N.Y., and London: Kennikat Press, 1971.

————. *The Writings of Margaret Fuller*. Ed. Mason Wade. New York, 1941.

Gardiner, William. *Sights in Italy*. London, 1847.

Garlik, Kenneth. *Sir Thomas Lawrence*. Boston: Boston Book & Art Shop, 1955.

Gebbia, Alessandro. *Citta teatrale: Lo spettacolo a Roma nelle impressioni dei viaggiatori americani 1760–1870*. Rome: Officina Edizioni, 1985.

Gell, Sir William. *The Topography of Rome and its Vicinity*. London: Saunders & Otley, 1834.

Gerdts, William H. "Washington Allston and the German Romantic Classicists in Rome." *Art Quarterly* 32, no. 1 (1969): 167–96.

Gerdts, William H., and Theodore E. Stebbins, Jr. *"A Man of Genius": The Art of Washington Allston (1779–1843)*. Boston: Museum of Fine Arts, 1979.

Gibbes, Robert. *A Memoir of James De Veaux, of Charleston, S.C.: Member of the National Academy of Design of New-York*. Columbia, 1846.

Gillespie, William Mitchell. *Rome as Seen by a New Yorker in 1843–4*. New York: Wiley & Putnam, 1845.

Goethe, Johann Wolfgang von. *Italian Journey, 1786–1788*. Ed. and trans. W. H. Auden and Elizabeth May. New York: Random House (Pantheon Books), 1962.

Goggio, Emilio. "Italy and Some of Her Early American Commentators," *Italica* 10 (March 1933): 4–10.

Grant, Michael. *The Roman Forum*. New York: Macmillan, 1970.

Greeley, Horace. *Glances at Europe*. New York, 1851.

Green, Edwin L. "Middleton, John Izard." In *Dictionary of American Biography*, edited by Dumas Malone, VI, 601–2. New York: Charles Scribner's Sons.

Greene, George Washington. "Historical Romance in Italy." *North American Review* 34(1838): 325–40.

Greenwood, Grace [Sara Lippincott]. *Haps and Mishaps of a Tour in Europe*. Boston: Ticknor, Reed & Fields, 1854.

———. *A Year Abroad: Stories and Sights in France and Italy*. Edinburgh: William Oliphant, 1870.

Griffin, Edmund Dorr. *A Tour through Italy and Switzerland in 1829 in the Remains of the Rev. Edmund D. Griffin*. Ed. Francis Griffin. 2 vols. New York, 1831.

Groseclose, Barbara S. "Harriet Hosmer's Tomb to Judith Falconnet: Death and the Maiden." *American Art Journal* 12 (Spring 1980): 78–89.

Hakewill, James. *A Picturesque Tour of Italy, From Drawings Made in 1816–1817*. London, 1820.

Hall, Fanny W. *Rambles in Europe; or a Tour through France, Italy, Switzerland, Great Britain, and Ireland, in 1836*. 2 vols. New York: French, 1838.

Hall, J. R. *The Italian Journal of Samuel Rogers*. London, 1956.

Hammond, J. *The Camera Obscura: A Chronicle*. Bristol, 1981.

Hardie, Martin. *Watercolour Painting in Britain*. Vol. 1, *The Eighteenth Century*. Vol. 2, *The Romantic Period*. Ed. Dudley Snelgrove, Jonathan Mayne, and Basil Taylor. Batsford, 1968.

Hare, Augustus J. C. *Days Near Rome*. 2 vols. London: Daldy, Isbister & Co., 1875.

Hawthorne, Nathaniel. *The Marble Faun or the Romance of Monte Beni*. 2 vols. Boston: Ticknor & Fields, 1860.

———. *Passages from the French and Italian Note-Books*. Riverside ed. Boston, 1883.

Hazlitt, William. *Notes of a Journey through France and Italy*. London: Hunt & Clarke, 1826.

Head, Sir George. *Rome: A Tour of Many Days*. 3 vols. London, 1849.

Headley, Joel T. *Letters from Italy*. New York: Wiley & Putnam, 1847.

Heine, Heinrich. *Pictures of Travel*. Trans. Charles Godfrey Leland. 2 vols. London: William Heinemann, 1898.

Herold, J. Christopher. *Mistress to an Age: A Life of Madame de Staël*. Indianapolis: Bobbs-Merrill, 1958.

Herriot, Edouard. *Madame Récamier*. Trans. Alys Hallard. 2 vols. New York and London: G. P. Putnam/William Heinemann, 1906.

Hewins, Amasa. *Hewin's Journal; A Boston Portrait-Painter Visits Italy, 1830–1833*. Ed. Francis W. Allen. Boston, n.d.

Hillard, George Stillman. *Six Months in Italy*. 2 vols. Boston: Ticknor, Reed & Fields, 1834.

Hoare, Richard Colt. *A Classical Tour through Italy and Sicily.* 2 vols. London: J. Mawman, 1819.

Holbrook, Silas P. *Sketches By a Traveller.* Boston, 1830.

Hosmer, Harriet. *Harriet Hosmer, Letters and Memoirs.* Ed. Cornelia Carr. New York: Moffat, Yard & Co., 1912.

Howe, Julia Ward. *Reminiscences, 1819–1899.* Boston, 1899.

Howe, M. A. DeWolfe. *The Life and Letters of George Bancroft.* New York, 1908.

Humphreys, Henry Noel. *Rome, and its Surrounding Scenery.* London, 1840.

Iannattoni, Livio. *Roma e gli Inglesi.* Rome: Atalantica, 1945.

Irving, Washington. *The Complete Works of Washington Irving: Journals and Notebooks.* Vol. 1 (1803–6). Ed. Nathalia Wright. Madison: University of Wisconsin Press, 1969.

———. *Notes and Journal of Travel in Europe: 1804–1805.* New York, 1921.

Izard, Ralph. *Correspondence.* Ed. Anne I. Deas. New York, 1844.

Jaffe, Irma B., ed. *The Italian Presence in American Art, 1760–1860.* New York: Fordham University Press / Rome: Istituto della Enciclopedia Italiana, 1989.

James, John. *Sketches of Travels in Sicily, Italy and France, in a Series of Letters Addressed to a Friend in the United States.* Albany: Packard & van Benthuysen, 1820.

Jameson, Anna. *Diary of an Ennuyée.* London: H. Colburn, 1826.

Jarves, James Jackson. *Italian Sights and Papal Principles Seen through American Spectacles.* New York, 1856.

Jewett, Isaac Appleton. *Passages in Foreign Travel.* Vol. 2. Boston: Little & Brown, 1838.

Keaveney, Raymond. *Views of Rome from the Thomas Ashby Collection in the Vatican Library.* London: Scala Books for the Smithsonian Institution and the Biblioteca Apostolica Vaticana, 1988.

Kemble, Frances (Fanny) Ann. *The Year of Consolation.* 2 vols. Hartford, 1851.

Kip, William Ingraham. *The Christmas Holydays in Rome.* New York, 1846.

Kirby, Paul Franklin. *The Grand Tour in Italy (1700–1800).* New York: E. P. Dutton, 1869.

Klenze, Camillo von. *The Interpretation of Italy during the Last Two Centuries.* Chicago: University of Chicago Press, 1907.

Laing, Samuel. *Notes of a Traveller, on the Social and Political State of France, Prussia, Switzerland, Italy and Other Parts of Europe, during the Present Century.* London: Longman, Brown, Green & Longmans, 1842.

Larg, David Glass. *Madame de Staël: la seconde vie, 1800–1807.* Paris: Champion, 1928.

Leland, Henry Perry. *Americans in Rome.* New York, 1863.

Lester, Charles Edwards. *My Consulship.* New York, 1853.

Lewis, Kenneth E., and Donald L. Hardesty. *Middleton Place: Initial Archaeological Investigations at an Ashley River Rice Plantation.* Columbia, S.C.: South Carolina Institute of Archaeology and Anthropology, 1979.

Liversidge, Michael, and Catherine Edwards, eds. *Imaging Rome: British Artists and Rome in the Nineteenth Century.* London: Merrell Holberton, 1996.

Longfellow, Henry Wadsworth. *Letters of Henry Wadsworth Longfellow.* Vol. 1. Cambridge, Mass.: Harvard University Press (Belknap Press), 1966.

———. *Longfellow's Poetical Works: Voices of the Night, Ballads and Other Poems.* Vol. 1. Boston and New York: Houghton, Mifflin, 1886.

———. *Outre-Mer: A Pilgrimage Beyond the Sea, 1834–35.* Boston and New York: Houghton, Mifflin, 1886.

Lowell, James Russell. *Fireside Travels.* Cambridge: Riverside Press, 1904.

Lyman, Theodore Jr. *The Political State of Italy.* Boston: Wells & Lilly, 1820.

MacGavock, Randal W. *A Tennessean Abroad or, Letters from Europe, Africa, and Asia.* New York, 1854.

Mac Veagh, Mrs. Charles. *Fountains of Papal Rome.* New York: Charles Scribner's Sons, 1915.

Mainardi, Patricia, Graham Bader, Thomas Beischer, et al. *The Persistence of Classicism.* Williamstown, Mass.: Sterling and Francine Clark Art Institute, 1995.

Manigault, Harriet. *The Diary of Harriet Manigault, 1813–1816.* Rockland, Maine, 1976.

Martyn, Thomas. *The Gentleman's Guide in his Tour through Italy.* London: G. Kearsley, 1787.

Masson, Georgina. *The Companion Guide to Rome.* New York: Harper & Row, 1965.

Maugham, Neville H. *The Book of Italian Travel (1580–1900).* New York, 1903.

Meade, C. Wade. *Ruins of Rome: A Guide to the Classical Antiquities.* Ruston, La.: Palatine, 1980.

Middleton, Alicia Hopton. *Life in Carolina and New England during the Nineteenth Century . . . .* Bristol, R.I., 1929.

Middleton, John Izard. *Grecian Remains in Italy: A Description of Cyclopian Walls, and of Roman Antiquities, with Typographical and Picturesque Views of Ancient Latium.* London: Edward Orme, 1812.

Middleton Family Papers. Middleton Place Foundation, Charleston, S.C.

Miles, Edwin A. "Young American Nation and the Classical World." *Journal of the History of Ideas* 35 (1974): 259–74.

Morgan, Dr. John. *The Journal of Dr. John Morgan of Philadelphia from the City of Rome to the City of London, 1764.* Philadelphia, 1907.

Morgan, Lady Sydney. *Italy.* 2 vols. New York: C. S. van Winckle, 1821.

Morse, Samuel F. B. *S. F. B. Morse, His Letters and Journals.* 2 vols. New York, 1914.

Murray, John. *Murray's Handbook of Rome and its Environs.* 7th ed. London: John Murray, 1864.

Nash, Ernest. *Pictorial Dictionary of Ancient Rome.* 2 vols. 2nd ed. New York: Praeger, 1968.

Nibby, Antonio. *Del foro romano, della via sacra, dell' anfiteatro flavio.* Rome: Poggioli, 1819.

———. *Roma antica.* 2 vols. Rome: Tipografia delle Belle Arti, 1838–39.

———. *Roma nell'anno MDCCCXXXVIII, parte seconda: Moderna.* 2 vols. Rome, 1839.

Nicolson, Harold. *Benjamin Constant.* Garden City, N.Y.: Doubleday, 1949.

Niebuhr, Barthold Georg. *History of Rome.* Trans. Julius Charles Hare and Connop Thirlwall. 3 vols. London: Taylor and Walton, 1837–44.

Nightingale, Florence. *Florence Nightingale in Rome: Letters Written in Rome in the Winter of 1847–1848.* Ed. Mary Keele. Philadelphia: American Philosophical Society, 1981.

Noble, Louis Legrand. *The Life and Works of Thomas Cole.* 1853. Reprint, ed. Elliott S. Vessell. Cambridge, Mass.: Harvard University Press, 1964.

Norton, Charles Eliot. "The First American Classical Archaeologist." *American Journal of Archaeology* 1 (January 1885): 3–9.

———. *The Letters of Charles Eliot Norton, with Biographical Comment by his Daughter Sara Norton and M. A. DeWolfe Howe.* 2 vols. Boston and New York, 1913.

———. *Notes of Travel and Study in Italy.* Boston: Ticknor & Fields, 1860.

O'Bryan, Michael. "Italy and the Southern Romantics." In *Rethinking the South,* edited by O'Bryan, 84–111. Baltimore: Johns Hopkins University Press, 1988.

Paget, R. F. *Central Italy: An Archaeological Guide.* Park Ridge, N.J.: Noyes Press, 1973.

Park, Roswell. *A Hand-Book for American Travellers in Europe.* New York: Clark, Austin & Smith, 1854.

Parkman, Francis. *Journals.* Vol. 1. Ed. Mason Wade. New York, 1947.

Parpagliolo, Luigi. *Italia (negli scrittori italiani e stranieri).* Vol. 1. Lazio, Rome, 1928.

Peale, Rembrandt. *Notes on Italy Written during a Tour in the Years 1829 and 1830.* Philadelphia: Carey & Lea, 1831.

Pearson, John. *Arena: The Story of the Coliseum.* New York: McGraw-Hill, 1973.

Piccolomini, Aeneas Silvius (Pope Pius II). *Memoirs of a Renaissance Pope.* Trans. Florence A. Gragg. Ed. Leona C. Gabel. New York: Capricorn, 1962.

Pine-Coffin, R. S. *Bibliography of British and American Travel in Italy to 1860.* Biblioteca di Bibliografia Italiana 86. Florence: Leo S. Olschki, 1974.

Pinto Surdi, Alessandra, and Cristina Penteriani Rossetti. *Americans in Rome, 1764–1870: A Descriptive Catalogue of the Exhibition Held in the Palazzo Antici Mattei* . . . . Rome: Centro di Studi Americani, 1984.

Prescott, William Hickling. *The Correspondence of W. H. Prescott.* Ed. Roger Wolcott. Boston: Houghton, 1927.

Preston, William C. *Reminiscences.* Ed. Minnie Clare Yarborough. Chapel Hill, N.C., 1933.

Prezzolini, Giuseppe. *Come gli Americani scoprirono l'Italia: 1750–1850.* Milan: Fratelli Treves, 1933.

Quennell, Peter. *The Colosseum.* New York: Newsweek, 1971.

Rapelje, George. *A Narrative of Excursions, Voyages, and Travels Performed at Different Periods in America, Europe, Asia, and Africa.* New York, 1834.

Ratcliff, Carter. "Allston and the Historic Landscape." *Art in America* 68 (1980): 97–104.

Récamier, Madame Juliette. *Memoirs and Correspondence of M. Récamier.* Ed. Amalie Lenormont. Boston: Knight & Millet, n.d.

Richardson, Edgar P., and Otto Wittmann Jr. *Travelers in Arcadia: American Artists in Italy, 1830–1875.* Detroit: Detroit Institute of Arts, 1951.

Rivas, Michele. "American Presence in Papal Rome." In Alessandra Pinto Surdi and Cristina Penteriani Rossetti, *Americans in Rome, 1764–1870: A Descriptive Catalogue of the Exhibition Held in the Palazzo Antici-Mattei . . . .* Rome: Centro di Studi Americani, 1984, Afterword, pp. 1–8.

Rives, Judith P. *Tales and Souvenirs of a Residence in Europe. By a Lady of Virginia.* Philadelphia, 1842.

Rogers, Samuel. *Italy: A Poem.* London: T. Cade, 1836.

Rutledge, Anna Wells. *Artists in the Life of Charleston: Through Colony and State from Restoration to Reconstruction.* Transactions of the American Philosophical Society, new series 39, no. 2. Philadelphia: American Philosophical Society, 1949.

Salamone, A. W. "The 19th Century Discovery of Italy: An Essay in American Cultural History; Prolegomena to a Historiographical Problem." *American Historical Review* 73 (1968): 1359–91.

Salmon, J. *An Historical Description of Ancient and Modern Rome . . . .* 2 vols. London: S. Gosnell, 1800.

Salvagnini, Francesco Alberto. *La Basilica di Sant'Andrea Delle Fratte.* 2nd ed. Rome: Basilica di S. Andrea delle Fratte, 1967.

Salvinetti, Holly Pinto. *American Artists Abroad: The European Experience in the 19th Century.* Roslyn, N.Y.: Nassau County Museum of Fine Art, 1985.

Sansom, Joseph. *Letters from Europe, during a Tour through Switzerland and Italy, in the Years 1801 and 1802.* 2 vols. Philadelphia: A. Bartram, 1805.

Sass, Henry. *A Journey to Rome and Naples, Performed in 1817: Giving an Account of the Present State of Society in Italy and Containing Observations on the Fine Arts.* New York: James Eastburn & Co., 1818.

Schauffler, Robert Haven, ed. *Through Italy with the Poets.* New York: Moffat, Yard & Co., 1908.

Schudt, Ludwig, and Oskar Pollak. *Le Guide di Roma: Materialien zu einer Geschichte der R'mischen Topographie.* 1930. Reprint, Westmead: Gregg International, 1971.

Scott, Leonora Cranch. *The Life and Letters of Christopher Pearse Cranch.* Boston and New York: Houghton Mifflin, 1917.

Sedgwick, Henry Dwight. *Madame Récamier: The Biography of a Flirt.* Indianapolis and New York: Bobbs-Merrill, 1940.

Serros, Richard. "The Influence of Travel Books: Samuel Rogers and J. M. W. Turner in Italy." In *The Anglo-American Artist in Italy, 1750–182,* edited by Corlette Rossiter Walker, 131–37. Santa Barbara: University Art Museum, University of California at Santa Barbara, 1982.

Shelley, Mary Wollstonecraft. *The Journals of Mary Shelley.* 2 vols. Ed. Paula Feldman. Oxford: Oxford University Press, 1987.

———. *The Letters of Mary W. Shelley.* Ed. Frederick Jones. Norman: University of Oklahoma Press, 1944.

———. *The Letters of Mary Wollstonecraft Shelley.* Vol. 1. Ed. Betty T. Bennett. Baltimore and London: Johns Hopkins University Press, 1980.

———. *Mary Shelley's Journal.* Ed. Frederick Jones. Norman: University of Oklahoma Press, 1947.

———. *Rambles in Germany and Italy, in 1840, 1842, and 1843.* 2 vols. London, 1844.

Shelley, Percy Bysshe. *The Letters of Percy Bysshe Shelley.* Vol. 1. Ed. R. Ingpen. London: I. Pitman, 1909.

Sherwood, Dolly. *Harriet Hosmer: American Sculptor, 1830–1908.* Columbia and London: University of Missouri Press, 1991.

Simond, Louis. *Switzerland; or, A Journal of a Residence in the Country in the Years 1817, 1818, and 1819.* Boston: Wells and Lilly, 1822.

———. *A Tour of Italy and Sicily.* London: Longman, Rees, Orme, Brown & Green, 1828.

Sloan, James. *Rambles in Italy in the Years 1816–17 by an American.* Baltimore: N. G. Maxwell, 1818.

Snow, W. *Handbook for the Baths of Lucca.* Pisa: Vannucchi, 1847.

Soria, Regina. *Dictionary of Nineteenth-Century American Artists in Italy, 1760–1914.* Rutherford, Madison and Teaneck: Fairleigh Dickinson University Press / London and Toronto: Associated University Presses, 1982.

Sperling, L. Joy. "Allston, Vanderlyn and the German Artistic Community in Rome, 1800–1810." In *The Anglo-American Artist in Italy, 1750–1820,* ed. Corlette Rossiter Walker, 115–24. Santa Barbara: University Art Museum, University of California at Santa Barbara, 1982.

Staël, Madame de (Anne Louise Germaine Necker, the Baroness de Staël-Holstein). *Corinne, or Italy.* Trans. and ed. Avriel H. Goldberger. New Brunswick, N.J. and London: Rutgers University Press, 1987.

———. *Correspondance Generale, VI: De "Corrine" vers "de l'Allemagne."* Ed. Beatrice W. Jasinski. Geneva: Klincksieck, 1993.

Starke, Mariana. *Letters from Italy, Between the Years 1792 and 1798 . . . .* 2 vols. London: R. Phillips, 1800.

———. *Travels in Europe for the Use of Travellers on the Continent.* 8th ed. Paris: A. W. Galignani, 1833.

Stebbins, Theodore E. Jr. *The Lure of Italy: American Artists and the Italian Experience, 1760–1914.* New York: Harry N. Abrams for Museum of Fine Arts, Boston, 1992.

Stendhal (Marie Henri Beyle). *A Roman Journal.* Ed. and trans. Haakon Chevalier. New York: Orion Press, 1957.

Stevens, Abel. *Madame de Staël: A Study of her Life and Times.* 2 vols. New York: Harper & Brothers, 1881.

Story, William Wetmore. *Graffiti d'Italia*. Edinburgh: Blackwood, 1868.

———. *Roba di Roma*. 1856. Reprint, 2 vols. Boston and New York: Houghton Mifflin, 1887.

Sumner, Charles. *Memoir and Letters of Charles Sumner*. Ed. Edward Lillie Peirce. 4 vols. Boston: Roberts, 1877–93.

Taine, Hippolyte. *Italy: Rome and Naples*. 1868. Reprint, trans. J. Durand. 4th ed. New York: Henry Holt, 1889.

Tappen, George. *Professional Observations on the Architecture of the Principal Ancient and Modern Buildings in France and Italy*. London, 1806.

Taylor, Bayard. *Views A-Foot, or Europe Seen, with Knapsack and Staff*. New York and London: G. P. Putnam, 1884.

Ticknor, Anna Eliot. *Life of Joseph Green Cogswell as Sketched in his Letters*. Cambridge, 1874.

Ticknor, George. *Life, Letters, and Journals*. 2 vols. Ed. George S. Hillard and Anna Ticknor. Boston: James Osgood, 1877.

Tomassetti, Giuseppe. *La Campagna Romana: antica, medioevale e moderna*. Vol. 2. Florence: Leo S. Olschki, 1979.

Topliff, Samuel. *Topliff's Travels: Letters from Abroad in the Years 1828–9*. Boston: Boston Athenaeum, 1906.

Tresoldi, Lucia. *Viaggatori tedeschi in Italia, 1452–1870: saggio bibliografico*. 2 vols. Rome, 1975.

Trollope, Mrs. Frances Milton. *A Visit to Italy*. 2 vols. London: Richard Bentley, 1842.

Tuckerman, Henry Theodore. *Italian Sketchbook by an American*. New York: J. C. Ricker, 1848.

———. *Rambles and Reveries*. New York: James Giffing, 1841.

Turner, J. H. *Revelations of Rome; Sketches of the Past and Present*. London and Dublin, 1868.

Twain, Mark [Samuel Clemens]. *Innocents Abroad or the New Pilgrims' Progress*. 2 vols. New York and London: Harper, 1911.

Vance, William L. *America's Rome: Volume One, Classical Rome*. 2 vols. New Haven and London: Yale University Press, 1989.

Vanderbilt, Kermit. *Charles Eliot Norton: Apostle of Culture in a Democracy*. Cambridge: Harvard University Press, 1959.

Varriano, John. *Rome: A Literary Companion*. London: John Murray, 1991.

Vasi, Mariano. *A New Picture of Rome and its Environs in the Form of an Itinerary*. London, 1819.

Vasi, Mariano, and Antonio Nibby. *Handbook of the New Guide of Rome and the Environs*. Rome: L. Piale, 1847.

Venn, John Archibald. *Alumni Cantabrigenses*. Cambridge: Cambridge University Press, 1922.

Waiblinger, Wilhelm. *Werke und Briefe*. vol. 1, *Gedichte* and vol. 4, *Reisebilder aus Italien*. Stuttgart: J. G. Cotta'sche Buchlandlung Nachfolger, 1980.

Ware, William. *Sketches of European Capitals*. Boston, 1851.

Watson, Wendy M. *Images of Italy: Photography in the Nineteenth Century*. South Hadley, Mass.: Mount Holyoke College Art Museum, 1980.

Whipple, Evangelina. *A Famous Corner of Tuscany*. London: Jerrolds, 1920.

White, Rev. Thomas H. *Fragments of Italy and the Rhineland*. London, 1841.

Williams, D. E. *The Life and Correspondence of Sir Thomas Lawrence*. 2 vols. London: Henry Colburn & Richard Bentley, 1831.

Williams, H. Noel. *Madame Récamier and her Friends*. London and New York: Harper & Brothers, 1901.

———. *Pencillings by the Way*. 3 vols. London: T. Werner Laurie, 1942.

Willis, Nathaniel Parker. *Dashes at Life with a Free Pencil*. New York, 1844.

Wilton, Andrew, and Ilaria Bignamini, eds. *Grand Tour: The Lure of Italy in the Eighteenth Century*. London: Tate Gallery Publishing, 1996.

Wittman, Otto, Jr. "Americans in Italy." *College Art Journal* 17 (1958): 284–93.

———. "The Attraction of Italy for American Painters." *Antiques* 85 (1964): 552–56.

———. "The Italian Experience (American Artists in Italy)." *American Quarterly* 4 (1952): 3–15.

Wollaston, George Hyde. *The Englishman in Italy: Being a Collection of Verses Written by Some of Those who have Loved Italy*. Oxford: Clarendon Press, 1909.

Woolson, Constance Fenimore. "Up the Ashley and Cooper." *Harper's Magazine* 52 (1875): 1–24.

Wordsworth, William. "The Pillar" and "At Rome." In *The Poetical Works of William Wordsworth*. Boston, 1982.

Wright, Nathalia. *American Novelists in Italy; The Discoverers: Allston to James*. Philadelphia: University of Pennsylvania Press, 1965.

Wynne, George. *Early Americans in Rome*. Rome: Dapco, 1966.

Index of Names

CHARLES R. MACK has been a member of the Department of Art at the University of South Carolina since 1970, where he is Louise Fry Scudder Professor of Art History and William J. Todd Professor of the Italian Renaissance. Mack teaches, researches, and writes about ancient and Renaissance art and architecture.

LYNN ROBERTSON is director of the University of South Carolina McKissick Museum. A contributor to *Gullah Images: The Art of Jonathan Green,* she has organized major national traveling exhibits and written catalogues on South Carolina art and folklife.